بِسْمِ ٱللَّهِ ٱلرَّحْمَٰنِ ٱلرَّحِيمِ

In the Name of God,

The All-Merciful, the Most Merciful

Forty Parables of The Holy Qurʾān

Shaykh Aḥmad Saad al-Azharī

Translated by

Khalid Williams

© 2025/1447 by Ihya Publishing
All rights reserved. No part of this publication may be reproduced, distributed, or transmitted in any form or by any means, including photocopying, recording, or other electronic or mechanical methods, without the prior written permission of the Ihya Publishing the Publisher.

ISBN 978-1-939256-24-9 (Paperback)

First Printing, 2025
Published by:
Ihya Publishing
P.O. Box 426
Alburtis, PA-18011

www.ihyapublishing.com
info@ihyapublishing.com

Author: Shaykh Ahmad Saad al-Azhari
Translator: Khalid Williams
Editor: Muhammad Isa Waley
Managing Editor: Athar Jatoi

Distributed by:
Mecca Books
www.meccabooks.com
info@meccabooks.com

IHYA
PUBLISHING

Ihya Publishing is a non-profit 501(c)(3) publishing house.

Contents

Author's Introduction 12
Parable 1: The State of the Hypocrites 20
Parable 2: How Showing Off Annuls Good Deeds 24
Parable 3: The Charity of the Sincere 30
Parable 4: The Biting Wind 36
Parable 5: The Orphan's Property Brings Terrible Torment 40
Parable 6: The Muḥammadan Light 46
Parable 7: The Victims of Delusion 50
Parable 8: Between Life and Death 56
Parable 9: The Expansion of Faith 62
Parable 10: The Narrowness of Unbelief 66
Parable 11: Good Land and Bad Land 70
Parable 12: The Panting Dog 76
Parable 13: The Weight of Pleasures 82
Parable 14: The Reality of Life in This World 88
Parable 15: An Apt Comparison 96
Parable 16: Holding On to Water 100
Parable 17: The Likeness of Truth and Falsehood 104
Parable 18: The Good Word and the Bad Word 108
Parable 19: The Powerless Idols 114
Parable 20: Breaking Promises 120
Parable 21: The Eternal Value of Deeds 124
Parable 22: Mercy to Parents 128
Parable 23: Between Miserliness and Extravagance 132
Parable 24: The Rolled-Up Pages 140
Parable 25: Worshiping Upon the Brink 144
Parable 26: The Light of the Heavens and the Earth 148
Parable 27: A Mirage in the Desert 154
Parable 28: The Waves of Darkness 160
Parable 29: Too Late for Regret 164
Parable 30: A Spiders House 168

Parable 31: The Slave Partners	174
Parable 32: The Illuminating Lamp	180
Parable 33: In the Service of Partners	184
Parable 34: The Lifestyle of Livestock	188
Parable 35: Like a Sapling that Grows Stout	196
Parable 36: The Backbiter	200
Parable 37: The Goodly Loan	206
Parable 38: The Effects of Neglecting the Revealed Law	210
Parable 39: Remembrance is the Life of the Heart	216
Parable 40: Form Without Substance	220
Conclusion	226
Bibliography	230

TRANSLITERATION KEY

ء، أ، إ	' (A slight catch in the breath. It is also used to indicate where the *hamza* has been dropped from the beginning of a word.)
ا	a, ā
ب	b
ت	t
ث	th (Should be pronounced as the *th* in *thin* or *thirst.*)
ج	j
ح	ḥ (Tensely breathed *h* sound.)
خ	kh (Pronounced like the *ch* in Scottish *loch* with the mouth hollowed to produce a full sound.)
د	d
ذ	dh (Should be pronounced as the *th* in *this* or *that.*)
ر	r
ز	z
س	s
ش	sh
ص	ṣ (A heavy *s* pronounced far back in the mouth with the mouth hollowed to produce a full sound.)
ض	ḍ (A heavy *d/dh* pronounced far back in the mouth with the mouth hollowed to produce a full sound.)
ط	ṭ (A heavy *t* pronounced far back in the mouth with the mouth hollowed to produce a full sound.)
ظ	ẓ (A heavy *dh* pronounced far back in the mouth with the mouth hollowed to produce a full sound.)
ع	ʿ, ʿa, ʿi, ʿu (Pronounced from the throat.)
غ	gh (Pronounced like a throaty French *r* with the mouth hollowed to produce a full sound.)
ف	f
ق	q (A guttural *q* sound with the mouth hollowed to produce a full sound.)
ك	k
ل	l
م	m
ن	n
و	w, ū, u.
ه	h
ي	y, ī, i

ﷺ	*Ṣalla 'Llāhu ʿalayhi wa sallam*—used following the mention of the Messenger Muḥammad, translated as, "May Allāh bless him and give him peace."
﵇	*ʿAlayhi 'l-salām*—used following the mention of a prophet or messenger of Allāh, translated as, "May the peace of Allāh be upon him."
﵁	*Raḍiya 'Llāhu ʿanhu*—used following the mention of a Companion of the Messenger ﷺ, translated as, "May Allāh be pleased with him."
﵂	*Raḍiya 'Llāhu ʿanhā*—used following the mention of a female Companion of the Messenger ﷺ, translated as, "May Allāh be pleased with her."
﵀	*Raḥimahu 'Llāh*—used following the mention of a scholar or pious individual, translated as, "May Allāh have mercy on him."
﵏	*Raḥimahumu 'Llāh*—used following the mention of more than one scholar or pious individual, translated as, "May Allāh have mercy on them."

These are the parables We set forth for humanity, but none will understand them except the people of knowledge.

Qur'ān 29:43

Author's Introduction

Praise be to God, Who transcends all equals and peers, all images and mental forms, and Who sent down upon His servant, our master Muḥammad ﷺ, a Book crowned with beauty, dumbfounding and silencing even the most eloquent of men. May perfect and enduring blessings and peace be upon our master and liege Muḥammad ﷺ, the spirit and embodiment of perfection, and the universal point of contact [with the Divine]; and upon his Family, Companions, and dutiful followers.

Now, God has revealed His Book for the enlightenment of those endowed with vision and reason, and as a reminder to the mindful. In it, He has adopted diverse modes of discourse to communicate with many different types of mentalities—commanding and forbidding, encouraging and dissuading, promising and threatening—all in elegant words and judicious language, sometimes treading the path of literalism and at other times following the way of metaphor. This is aimed at rousing the human soul so that the eye of vision and insight may open, and that the innermost secret heart may be polished with its meanings and teachings.

One of the most effective of those techniques is the use of parables. A parable is a valuable way of teaching and fixing concepts in the heart, because it shifts the focus from a purely abstract concept to a tangible image, a concrete reality in the mind. The use of parables is a time-honored tradition, a well-trodden path of the ancients. In the age of pagan ignorance, the Arabs made an art of it and had

مقدمة المؤلِّف

الحمدُ لله المنزه عن كل نظير و مثال، جلَّ عن كل صورة وخيال، أنزل على عبده سيدنا محمدٍ كتاباً المكلل بالجمال، فأسكت به ألسن الفصحاء عن كل مقال. والصلاة والسلام الأتمان الأدومان الأكملان على سيدنا ومولانا محمدٍ روح شخص الكمال، ومحل كُلِّ وصال، وآله وأصحابه وأتباعه ذوي النوال.

وبعد فقد أنزل الله كتابه للمستبصرين تبصرة، وللمتذكرين تذكرة و نوَّع فيه سُبُل البيان، لتعدد الأذهان. فأمر ونهى، ورغّب ورهّب، ووعد وأوعد. كلُّ ذلك بلفظ رشيق وقول محكم يسلكُ سننَ الحقيقة حينا وينهج نهج المجاز أحيانا، يستحث النفس الإنسانية كي تفتح عين البصر والبصيرة، وتجلو بمعانيه ومراميه السر والسريرة. ومن جملةِ هذه الطرق الناجعة، والأساليب النافعة ضربُ المثل الذي يُقرِّب المعقول، ويستميل العقول، ويشفي العقل السؤول.

لذا كان من أنجع وسائل التعليم وتمكين المعاني من القلب والعقل لأنه نقل للمعقول المجرد إلى صورة المحسوس المنضد حتى يصير كالصرح الممرد. و ضرب الأمثال سنة في الناس غابرة وطريقة بين الأقدمين سائرة حتى تفنن العرب

frequent recourse to it, as is recorded in books on the classical Arabic language. The great Imam Abū Hilāl al-ʿAskarī[1] compiled the parables of the Arabs and arranged them meticulously in his illustrious work *Jamharat al-amthāl* ("Multitude of Parables").

In lexical terms, the word *mathal* (parable, similitude) means a proof, a description, or an attribute. Our Lord says, *To God belongs the loftiest quality (*mathal*)* [Qur'ān 16:60], and He says, *A likeness (*mathal*) of the Garden* [Qur'ān 47:15], meaning its description. Its plural is *amthāl*.[2] The Holy Qur'ān is replete with parables of an eloquence that would outdo any human author, however articulate, illustrating elusive concepts with such clarity that nothing is left vague, and conveying abstruse ideas with such clarity that no uncertainty remains. Muḥammad ibn ʿAlī al-Ḥakīm al-Tirmidhī (d. 320/869) says:

> Parables are archetypes of wisdom for the illustration of things which lie outside the range of the visual and audial senses, guiding souls by reference to things which they have seen first-hand. One of the ways in which God directs His servants is by providing them with parables drawn from themselves, which they are in need of to comprehend and perceive those things which lie beyond their outward vision and hearing. Those who understand parables are called 'knowing' by God Most High in His Book.[3]

Those parables, which God provides in the Qur'ān, are a great blessing and favor from Him "by means of which the knowing may find direction and right guidance," as Abū Hilāl al-ʿAskarī says.

1: Ḥasan ibn Sahl Abū Hilāl al-ʿAskarī (d. 400/1010) was a philologist and poet from Khūzistan, southwestern Iran.
2: For more, see the entry on *m-th-l* in al-Murtaḍā al-Zabīdī's *Tāj al-ʿurūs*.
3: Al-Ḥakīm al-Tirmidhī, *al-Amthāl*.

في جاهليتهم في ضرب الأمثال وجعلوا لها موردا ومضربا واتسعوا في ذلك اتساعا سجلته كتب اللغة حتي جمع الإمام الكبير أبو هلال العسكري الأمثال العربية ورتبها ترتيبا دقيقا في كتابه الجليل الشأن، "جمهرة الأمثال".

والمَثَلُ في اللغة هو الحجة والحديث نفسه والصفة. قال ربنا: "**ولله المثل الأعلى**" وقال: "**مثل الجنة**" أي صفتها والجمع: أمثال. وللتوسع انظر مادة: مثل في تاج العروس للمرتضى الزبيدي. والقرآن الكريم مشحون بالأمثال التي تُزري بلاغتها بكل فصيح - تصور ما استعصى من المعاني تصويرا لا يبقى معه أدني خفاء، وتقرب ما غاب فلا يبقي معها أدنى غموض أو ريب. يقول الحكيم الترمذي محمد بن علي المتوفى سنة ٣٢٠ ه:

> فالأمثال نموذجات الحكمة لما غاب عن الأسماع والأبصار لتهدي النفوس بما أدركت عيانا فمن تدبير الله لعباده أن ضرب لهم الأمثال من أنفسهم لحاجتهم إليها ليعقلوا بها فيدركوا ما غاب عن أبصارهم وأسماعهم الظاهرة. فمن عقل الأمثال، سماه الله تعالى في كتابه عالما.[١]

وهذه الأمثال - التي ضربها الله في القران- نعمة ومنةٌ منه سبحانه "ينتهي إليها العارف فيرشد ويهتدي بهديها" فيتسدد كما قال أبو هلال العسكري وهي فوق ذلك "مع

١: الأمثال للترمذي

Moreover, "their succinctness allows them to communicate much in a few words, and they have a particular charm when employed during a speech." They are an essential tool for the man of letters, though mastered only by the skillful rhetorician. A speaker who lacks proficiency in them is not fully equipped, and one who uses them without proper knowledge will add nothing but confusion.

The subject of the parables of the Noble Qur'ān has been treated by a fair number of major scholars and eminent masters. These include al-Ḥakīm al-Tirmidhī in *al-Amthila fī al-Qur'ān wal-Sunna* ('Parables in the Qur'ān and Sunna'), although not comprehensively but only mentioning a small few; Ibn Qayyim al-Jawziyya,[4] but his work is arranged in a manner which is not reader-friendly; and Shaykh 'Abd al-Raḥmān Ḥasan Ḥabbanaka,[5] although the scope of his book is broader and treats the subject of Qur'ānic literary style in general, without devoting full attention to the subject of parables in all their forms. For this and for other reasons, I felt compelled—despite my inadequacies—to delve into the subject myself, and to contemplate, reflect, and discover. I studied the Manifest Book closely and found that it contains just over forty parables. I took the number as a good sign and asked God for replenishing grace; and I have compiled forty parables, studied their meanings, and summarized their contents, extracting some of their benefits and lessons and presenting their subtle teachings in plain language. This is particularly important given that we are in an age when a reader may well lose interest when a discourse goes on for too long, fleeing in despair when his mind becomes distracted.

These studies have their origin in reflections and lessons before the *Tarāwīḥ* prayer in the month of Ramaḍān 1437/2015, which I gave in thirty sections corresponding to the number of nights and days in the month, like the term prescribed to Moses for his meeting

4: Ibn Qayyim al-Jawziyya (d. 751/1350) was a major scholar of the Ḥanbalī school from Damascus.

5: 'Abd al-Raḥmān Ḥasan Ḥabbanaka al-Maydānī (d. 1425/2004) was a Syrian scholar.

إيجازها تعمل عمل الإطناب ولها روعة إذا برزت في أثناء الخطاب" يحتاج إليها الأديب ولا يملك ناصيتها إلا الأريب، من نَقَص حظه منها كان غير تامِّ الآلة ومَن استعملها دون معرفة زاد ضِغْثا على إبّالة.

وباب أمثال القرآن الكريم قد ولجه عدد لا بأس به من أكابر العلماء والسادة الفضلاء منهم الحكيم الترمذي لكنه لم يستقص بل ذكر عددا قليلا جدا في كتابه "الأمثال في القرآن والسنة" وابن قيم الجوزية لكنه لم يرتبها ترتيبا يسهل مأخذها والشيخ عبد الرحمن حسن حبنكه لكنه توسع في كتابه فكان نظره في الأدب القرآني عموما ولم يستوف موضوع الأمثال بكافة صوره . وقد دعاني كل هذا وغيره - على قلة متاع وعدم باع- أن ألجَ هذا المولج وأنظر وأتدبر وأستخرج، فأجلت النظر في الكتاب المبين فوجدت أمثاله زادت بقليل على الأربعين فاستبشرت بالعدد وسألت الله المدد وجمعت أربعين مثلا حررت معانيها وأوجزت الكلام على ما فيها، ناشرا بعض الفوائد واللطائف وميسرا العبارة في إيصال دقيق المعارف، خاصة أننا في زمان يتململ القارئ فيه إذا أطلت الحديث، ويتشتت ذهنه ويفر كالمستغيث.

وأصل هذه الأمثال خواطر ودروس كنت ألقيها قبيل تراويح شهر رمضان سنة ١٤٣٧ هـ جملتها ثلاثون بعدد ليالي الشهر وأيامه، وكأنها موعد موسى- قبل تمامه، فأتمها الله تعالى - فضلا منه ونعمةً- أربعين كما أتم لموسى ميقات ربه المُعين، فالحمد لله على ذلك. وقد أعدت النظر فيها مرارا وجمعت لها من كتب التفسير واللغة والتصوف وغيرها ما أحمضتُ - أي نوعت - به محتواها كي تغزر فائدتها ويخرج

with God before it was extended. Then by His grace and favor, God Most High completed it by extending it to a total of forty, just as He extended the duration fixed for Moses's meeting; so all praise be to God for that. I have reviewed the material several times and added to it from books on Qur'ānic exegesis, language, Sufism, and other branches of knowledge in order to broaden the scope of the content and maximize its benefit, so that readers may find something to interest them.

I have previously published a summary of the meanings of the Holy Qur'ān, entitled *Irshād dhawī al-albāb*, in Arabic and English.[6] The intention—if God permits—is to publish these parables in a bilingual Arabic and English edition as well, so that more readers may benefit from them and learners may view both texts and enjoy the beauty of both languages.

While praising and thanking God Most High for His aid, I ask Him, Majestic and Glorious is He, to grace this book with the fullness of light; to make it well-known everywhere, from east to west; to bring through it benefit to every seeker and profit to every lover; to make this work, and those which preceded it, a shining light before its author on the Day of Resurrection; and to extend any reward for it to my teachers, my parents, my wife, my children, and to me after all of them. Truly He is the Bestower of every gift, the Ultimate Object of all hope.

By the most weak and needy one,

Dr. Aḥmad ibn Muḥammad Saad al-Azharī al-Ḥasanī al-Mālikī
Birmingham, 27th February 2018.

6: Published in a dual Arabic and English edition with the title *Contemplating the Quran: A Thematic Thirty-Part Commentary on the Noble Quran* ([Newport], 2017).

قاريها بشيء ذي بال.

وكما سبق وأخرجت مختصرا لمعاني القرآن الكريم أسميته "إرشاد ذوي الألباب" باللغتين، فالنية بإذن الله أن تطبع هذه الأمثال باللغتين العربية والإنجليزية لينتفع بها أكبر عدد من القراء وينظر المتعلم في النصين فيرى جمال اللغتين.

و أنني إذ أحمد الله تعالى على توفيقه أسأله جلَّ شأنه أن يتمَّ نورَها، وينشرَ في المشرقينِ والمغربينِ ذكرَها، وينفعَ بها كل محبِّ ويفيد منها كل راغب وأن يجعل هذا العمل - مع ما سبقه- نورا بين يدي كاتبه يوم القيامة، وأن يجري أجره لأشياخي ووالداي وزوجي وأولادي ولي من بعدهم إنه وليُّ كل عطاء، ومنتهى كلّ رجاء.

وكتبه الفقير الأضعف

د. أحمد بن محمد سعد الأزهري الحسني المالكي
في برمنكهام ٢٧ من فبراير ٢٠١٨

Parable 1: The State of the Hypocrites
Sūrat al-Baqara (2), Verses 17-18

Their likeness is as that of someone who kindled a fire, and when it radiated all about him, God took away their light and left them in darknesses, unable to see. Deaf, dumb, and blind, they shall not return.

This parable alludes to the state of the hypocrites. The sūra opens with a description of the states of those who received the divine Message and their various factions, clarifying that there are three of them: the believers, the unbelievers, and the hypocrites. Because of the special danger of the hypocrites, several verses are spent on describing them in detail, followed by this parable which presents the image of their state in a tangible form.

The parable here likens the state of the hypocrites—how they adopt Islam outwardly while not benefiting from it even after its merit and light is made manifest—to a man who lights a fire for himself, having dire need of it, and then when the fire puts forth light and illuminates the surroundings, God takes away the light, meaning that He extinguishes it, and the man remains in pitch-black darkness, bereft of benefit.

The verse contains several fine rhetorical features, including:

(1) His words *unable to see* emphasize how the sensation of darkness after light is more distressing than entering darkness to begin with.

المَثَلُ الأَوّل: حالُ المنافقين
سورة البقرة الآية: (١٧)

﴿مَثلُهُم كَمَثَلِ الذي اسْتَوْقَدَ ناراً فَلَمَّا أَضاءَتْ مَا حَوْلَهُ ذَهَبَ اللهُ بِنُوْرِهِمْ وَ تَرَكَهُمْ فِي ظُلُماتٍ لا يُبْصِرُوْن﴾

الإشارةُ في هذا المَثَلِ لِحالِ المُنَافِقِينَ، فَقَد افتُتِحَت السُّورةُ بالحَديثِ عَن أحوالِ المُتلَقّينَ للرِّسَالةِ وأَصنَافِهِم وَأَوْضَحَتْ أَنَّهُم على أَصنَافٍ ثلاثةٍ: المؤْمِنونَ والكَافِرون والمنافقون. ولِخُطُورةِ المُنَافِقينَ فَصَّلَت الآيَاتُ أوْصافَهُم ثم أَتْبَعَت ذلك بهذا المَثَلِ الذي يَجْعَلُ المُتَخَيَّلَ في حَقّهِم في صورة المشاهدِ المحسوس.

والمَثَلُ هُنا هو تشبيهُ حَالِ المُنافقينَ في تَعَرُّضِهِم للإسلامِ في الظاهِرِ مع عدم الاستفادة منه بعدَ ظُهُورِ فضله وَنُورِه بحالِ رَجُلٍ أَوقَد لنفسه نارا، اشتدت حَاجَتُهُ إليها فَلَمّا أَضاءت النارُ وَظَهرَ نورها وأَبانَتْ ما حَولَهَا من الجِهات، أَذَهَبَ اللهُ ذلكَ النّورَ أي أَطْفَأَهُ وبَقِيَ ذلك الرجُلُ في ظَلَامٍ دَامِسٍ لا يَنْتَفِعُ بِشيءٍ.

وفي الآيةِ جَمَاليّاتُ بلاغية مِنها:

(2) God Most High describes the effect of the fire by saying, *it radiated* (*aḍā'at*), implying that their inner beings were not illuminated and no benefit occurred, which is why He does not say, "it lit" (*anārat*).[7] Then when He wants to clarify what was taken away, He says, *God took away their light*, not "their radiance", choosing the word 'light' (*nūr*) to symbolize Islam because it is more fitting and apt, since the removal of light means the total removal of radiance on both the sensorial and spiritual levels, outwardly and inwardly, so that the person ends up groping in total darkness.

(3) God Most High says, *and left them in darknesses*, in the plural rather than "in darkness", in the singular, in order to stress the intensity of the darkness and the manifold states of misguidance into which the hypocrites are plunged, any one of which could be considered to be darkness on its own. These include the state of unbelief, the state of uncertainty, the state of deceit, and the state of mockery.

(4) This parable is a precise depiction of the adverse psychological effect that hypocrisy has upon the hypocrites, through comparing their state with that of the person in the parable. They cannot benefit from goodness when it appears, because the faith which they display to the believers when they meet them vanishes when they return to their devils and are alone with them. The effect of unbelief becomes more entrenched in them than it was before, just as when somebody lights a fire and then loses the light, his efforts come to nothing and the effect of the darkness on him becomes ever stronger, until he loses completely the ability to see.

7: This is based on the distinction between *nūr*, meaning the essence of light itself, and *ḍaw'*, meaning the radiance and effulgence of *nūr*.

(١) أنّ قَوله (لا يُبصِرون) تأكيدٌ على أن الإحساس بالظُلمةِ بعد النور أشدُّ إيْلَاما من الدخولِ بالظُلْمة ابتداءً.

(٢) أنَّ الله تعالى عبَّرَ عن أثَرِ النّار فقال: (أضاءت) إشارة لعدمِ استنارة بواطنهم وعدَمِ حُصولِ النّفع فلم يقل (أنارَت) ثم لمّا أرادَ أن يُوَضِّحَ مَا ذَهَبَ منها، قال: (**ذَهَبَ اللهُ بنورهم**) ولم يَقُلْ بضوئهم، فاختار لفظ النور إشارةً للإسلام لأنّه أنسب وأوقع ولأن ذهاب النور فيه معنى ذهاب الضوء بالكلية حسا ومعنى، ظاهرا وباطنا فيبقى صاحبه نُهبة التخبط.

(٣) أن الله تعالى قال: (**وتركهم في ظُلُماتٍ**) بصيغة الجمع، ولم يقُلْ (في ظُلْمَةٍ) بالإفراد، بيانا لشدّة الظُلمةِ وتعدُدِ أحوال الضلالة التي تعتري المُنافقين والتي يصلح كل واحدٍ منها أنْ يكُونَ ظُلمَة مستقلةً، فمنها: حالُ الكفرِ وحال الترددِ وحال الكذب وحالُ الاستهزاءِ.

(٤) دِقّةُ التّصْويرِ للأَثرِ النّفْسيِّ القَبيحِ الذي يَترُكُهُ النِّفاقُ عَلى المُنَافِقِ مِنْ خِلالِ النَّظرِ في وَجهِ الشَّبهِ بين حالِهم وبينَ المثَلِ المذكورِ، حيثُ ينعدمُ انتفاعُهم بالخير بعد ظهوره، فإن إظهارهم للإيمان عند لقيا المؤمنين تُنقضُ بعودتهم إلى شياطينهم وخلوهم بهم فَيرسُخُ أثرُ الكفرِ فيهم ويصيرُ أشدَّ من ذي قبل، كحال مستوقد النار الذي يفقد النورَ بعدَ وجوده فيخيب سعيهُ ويصير أثر الظلمة عليه أقوى حتى أنَهُ يفقد القدرة على الإبصار بالكلية.

Parable 2: How Showing Off Annuls Good Deeds

Sūrat al-Baqara (2), Verse 264

O you who believe, do not annul your acts of charity with reminders of your generosity or injury, like he who spends his wealth to show off to people and believes not in God and the Last Day. His likeness is as that of a smooth rock on which there is soil: a downpour strikes it and leaves it bare. They have no power over anything that they have earned; and God guides not the disbelieving folk.

This parable depicts the state of those who act hypocritically in order to win praise from other people, rather than in hope of pleasing God Most High and with faith in Him. It likens them to a smooth rock with a layer of soil upon it which to the onlooker appears to be arable land; but when he sows it and rain falls upon it the water washes the soil away, leaving nothing behind, and his hopes are dashed.

This parable is a very effective depiction of the vileness of ostentation and acting for the sake of pleasing other people and oneself. It illustrates that the show-off's mentality is superficial and limited, because if his mentality was deep enough for sincerity and real devotion, he would realize that the true purpose of charity is to purify the soul from the pollution of attachments to immediate gratification, one of the most significant of which is praise from other people, and to attach it instead to God, the All-Generous Who gives without limit or measure; and to make the notion of virtue take root in the

المَثَلُ الثّاني: آثار الرياء في إبطال الأعمال سورةُ البقرة الآية (٢٦٤)

﴿ يأيُّها الذينَ آمنُوا لا تُبْطِلوا صَدَقَاتِكُم بِالمَنّ والأَذَى كَالَّذي يُنْفِقُ مَالَهُ رِئَاء النَّاسِ ولا يُؤْمِنُ بالله واليَوْمِ الآخِرِ فَمَثَلُهُ كَمَثَلِ صَفْوَانٍ عَلَيْهِ تُرَابٌ فَأَصَابَهُ وَابِلٌ فتركَهُ صَلْداً لا يقْدِرُون عَلى شيْءٍ مِّمَّا كَسَبُوا واللهُ لا يَهْدي القَوْمَ الكٰفِرِينَ ﴾

هذا تشبيهٌ تَمثِيلِيّ، مَثَّلَ فيه حالَ الذي يُنفِقُ طلبا لمَحْمَدَةِ النّاس لا رجاء مرضاةِ الله تعالى وإيمانا به بحجرٍ قاسٍ أَمْلَسٍ تعلوه طَبَقةٌ من الترابِ، يظُنُّه الرائي تُربَةً كريمةً صالحةً للبذرِ فإذا زرعهُ وأصابَهُ المَطرُ جرفَ المَطرُ ذلك التُّرابَ ولمْ يُبقِ عليه شيئا فيَخِيبُ الأملُ.

وهذا المَثلُ ذو أَثَرٍ عَظِيمٍ في تَقبيحِ الرّياءِ والعَمَلِ من أجلِ الناسِ للنفوس، وبيانِ أنَّ عقلية المُرائي عقلية سطحيةٌ محدودةٌ لأَنَّها لَو تَعَمَّقتْ في معنى الصّدقةِ والبَذْلِ لَعَلِمَتْ أَنَّ المعنى الحقيقيَّ للعَطاء هو تَطْهيرُ النَّفس من أوضارِ التَّعلقِ بالمَنَافِعِ العَاجِلَةْ ومِن أَهَمِّهَا المَدحُ، وربطُهَا بالله الكَريمِ الذي يعطي بلا حدٍّ ولا عدٍّ، وتَجْذِيرُ مَعْنَى الخَيْرِ فيها كي

soul so that it becomes like good land which produces crops for all without expecting thanks or reward.

The soul of the show-off, contrastingly, is hard like rock, and so the effect of virtuous action cannot break through to its depths due to its bad intention. It might succeed in fooling people for a while with a semblance of virtue, but its true nature will quickly come to the surface, just as the soil atop that rock will be washed away by the first drops of rain.

Other lessons of this parable include:

(1) It shows that the show-off will not benefit from the charity he gives, just as barren rock does not benefit from the dust that sits on top of it; and it illustrates the severity of his loss, for he will lose both his wealth and his reward. Hence God says, *They have no power over anything that they have earned.*

(2) It illustrates the grace that God Most High extends to the show-off, despite his ostentation, by concealing his condition as the soil conceals that rock, while also warning him that this concealment is only temporary and will not last forever. This encourages him to rectify his intention and hasten to repent.

(3) It indicates the danger of judging people by outward appearances. Many an attractive exterior conceals a foul interior; and often a person's appearance may displease people although beneath it there is a pleasant soul filled with goodness. "Many a dusty, disheveled man in rags is turned away from doors—yet if he swore an oath by God, God would see it fulfilled," as the Messenger of God ﷺ said. Imam Ibn Mājah narrates in his *Sunan*[8] on the authority of Muʿādh ibn Jabal ﷺ that the Messenger of God ﷺ said, "Shall I tell you of the kings of Paradise?" Muʿādh replied, "Yes, do." He said, "A weak, oppressed man dressed in rags, noticed by no one— yet if he swore an oath by God, God would see it fulfilled."

8: Ibn Mājah, *Sunan* 4115.

تَصيرَ كالأَرضِ الطّيبةِ تُنبتُ لِكُلِّ أحدٍ دونَ انتظار شكرٍ أوْ جَزاء.

أما نَفسُ المُرائي، فَهيَ جَامِدةٌ كالحَجرْ، لا يتعدى أثرُ فِعالِ الخَيرِ إلى باطِنِها لفَسَادِ نيتها، قَدْ تَنْجَحُ في خِدَاعِ الناسِ بُرْهَةً من الزّمانِ مُتَظاهِرة بفِعْلِ الخَيْر، لَكنْ سَرْعَانَ ما تَظهرُ حقيقَتُها مثلَ التُّرابِ الذي يَعلُو وجهَ ذلك الحَجَرَ فيزولُ بأَوَّلِ قَطرةِ مَطَرٍ.

وِمنْ فَوائِدِ ضَربِ هَذا المَثَلِ إضافة لِما سَبَقَ:

(١) بَيانُ عَدَمِ انْتِفَاعِ المُرائِي بِنَفقَتهِ كما لا ينْتَفِعُ الحَجرُ الأملسُ الجامدُ بالغُبَارِ الذي عليه وإظْهارُ شدةِ خَسَارَتِهِ إذْ إنه يخسرُ المَالَ والثوَاب مَعا ولذا قَالَ: "**لا يَقدِرون على شيءٍ مما كسبوا**."

(٢) إظهارُ مِنّةِ الله تعالى على هذا المُرائي - رُغْمَ رياءه- بأَنْ سَترَ حَالَهُ كما يسْتُرُ التُّرابُ ذلك الحجرَ، معَ تَخويفِهِ بأَن ذلكَ السترَ آنِيٌّ لا ديمومةَ له، ومِن ثَمَّ تحفيزُهُ ودَفعهُ إلى إصلاحِ نيَّتهِ والمُسارعةِ بالتوبة.

(٣) الإشارةُ إلى خُطورةِ الحُكمِ على الظاهِرِ من الناس، فَكَمْ مِن زينَةٍ ظاهِرَةٍ تُخفي خبيئةً خبيثةً وكم مِن ظاهرٍ لا يُحبه الناس يُخفي بين جوانبهِ نفساً طيبةً عامرةً بالخيرِ، ورُبَّ أشعثَ أغْبَرَ ذي طمرين مَدفوعٍ بالأبواب لو أقسمَ على الله لأبره كما قال صاحبُ الرسالة صلوات الله عليه وسلامه وقد أخرجَ الإمام ابن ماجة في سننه مِن حديث معاذِ بن

The eminent Imam ʿAllāma Sayyid ʿAbd al-Raḥmān ibn ʿAbd Allāh Balfaqīh al-Bā ʿAlawī (d. 1162/1749) says in his poem *Rashafāt ahl al-kamāl*:

How many a poor man is hidden amid people,
Who is filled with the purest of certitude,
Disparaged by people, dressed in two rags,
Yet in God's sight he is high and mighty.
Many an unknown man is neglected by all,
Ignored till he passes away in obscurity.
Yet he was the one who rescued all the hopeful,
Most excellent in his character and states.

جبلٍ رضي الله عنه أن رسول الله صلى الله عليه وسلم قال: ألا أُخبرِكَ عن ملُوكِ الجنةِ؟ قلت: بلى. قال: رجلٌ ضعيفٌ مستَضَعفٌ ذو طِمرينِ لا يؤبهُ له لو أقسم على الله لأبرَّه.

وفي هذا المعنى يقول الإمام الجليل العلامة السيد عبد الرحمن بن عبد الله بلفقيه الباعلوي (١٠٨٩ - ١١٦٢ هـ) في منظومته المسماة برشفات أهل الكمال:

فَكَمْ خَفي في الناس مِن مسكينِ
قد امتلا من صفوَةِ اليقينِ
وهــانَ بين الناس ذو طِمــرَيْنِ
وهو لدى الحــقِّ عظيمٌ عال
وكَمْ أضــاع النَّــاسُ من مجهــولِ
وفاتَ حتى مــاتَ في الخُمولِ
وهوَ غياثُ كلِّ ذي مــأمولِ
في أفضــل الخِصــالِ والأَحــوالِ

Parable 3: The Charity of the Sincere
Sūrat al-Baqara (2), Verse 265

But the parable of those who spend their wealth seeking God's good pleasure, with certitude in their souls, is as the likeness of a garden upon a hill. A downpour strikes it, and it yields its produce twofold; and if no downpour strikes it, then drizzle. And God sees all that you do.

This parable presents us with an image in opposition to the previous one, depicting the state of the people of virtue and merit who give charity in the right way. On the one hand, they donate their wealth in pursuit of God's good pleasure; on the other, their donations come from souls which are stable and certain, harboring no irresoluteness in the ways of righteousness, nor paying heed to any impulses toward avarice from other quarters. The parable compares them to a thriving orchard upon a hill, exposed to rain at all times thanks to its favorable location. If a downpour of heavy rain strikes it, its yield will double and its yield will grow all the more; and even if it does not receive beneficial heavy rain, it will at least receive a drizzle of rain, which will suffice it thanks to its good soil and elevated position, and so it will produce its regular yield. In either case it is fruitful.

So it is with the people of sincerity and certitude. If their donations are large, God Most High causes them to grow and double; if they are small in material terms, God accepts them from them and makes them great in spiritual terms, because they have originated

المَثَلُ الثالِثُ: نفقات الصادقين
سورةُ البَقَرة الآية (٢٦٥)

﴿ وَمَثَلُ الذينَ يُنْفِقُونَ أَمْوَالَهُمْ ابْتِغَآءَ مَرْضَاتِ اللهِ وتَثْبِيتاً مِنْ أَنفُسِهِم كَمَثَلِ جَنَّةٍ بِرَبْوَةٍ أَصَابَهَا وَابِلٌ فئاتَتْ أُكُلَهَا ضِعْفَيْنِ فَإنْ لَمْ يُصِبْهَا وَابِلٌ فَطَلٌّ واللهُ بِمَا تَعْمَلونَ بَصِيرٌ ﴾

هذَا المثلُ يُبْرِزُ لنا صورةً مُضادةً للصورةِ السابِقَةِ، فهو يُمَثِّلُ حَالَ أصحاب الخيرِ والفضل ممن ينبعثُ الإنفاقُ من نُفُوسِهِم على وجهِهِ الصحيحِ- فيُنفِقُونَ أموالهُمْ طلباً لمرضاةِ الله مِنْ جهةٍ، وتخرجُ نَفَقاتُهم مِنْ نُفُوسٍ ثابتةٍ راسخَةٍ لا تترددُ في وُجوهِ البرِّ ولا تستمع لخواطِر الشُّح من جهةٍ أُخرى- بحال حديقةٍ زاهرةٍ فى أعلى ربوة تتعرض للمطر على كل حالٍ بسبب حُسن موقعها، فإن أصابها الوابل وهو المطرُ الشديد يتضاعف ثمرها ويزكوا نتاجها وإن لم ينلها المطر الشديد النافعُ، ينالها الطلُّ وهو المطرِ القليل الذي يكفيها لطيب تربتها وارتفاع مكانها فتؤتي أُكلها أيضا كعادتها، فهي مثمرة في الحالين.

وكذلك حال أهل الإخلاص واليقين، إن كانت نفقاتهم عظيمة زكاها الله تعالى وضاعفها، وإن كانت قليلة

from souls which have been made accustomed to charity and virtue until loftiness has become their way of life. Donating wealth with sincerity is one of the greatest ways of making obedience firmly rooted in the soul, because it purifies it from selfishness and material attachment.

The beautiful rhetorical features of this parable include:

(1) It gives consolation to the people of sincerity, telling them that their deeds will never lack benefit, because they are grown from roots that are solid and good. A solid root is the foundation of all that it good. But these verses also encourage us to ascend and do more, so that the fruits of our deeds may grow and double. As one of the gnostics said, "Actions grow to the extent that states are purified; states are purified to the extent that one attains realization in the stations of alighting, i.e., the stations of certitude. When a person truly alights in the stations of certitude, all of his actions will be mighty ones."[9]

(2) It compares a virtuous, generous soul to a garden, and compares its rising to the station of sincerity to a hill. In that station, everything that comes from it is good; and even if its effect is not a downpour it will at least be a shower. This is a splendid image which augments the beauty of the garden, whose fruit becomes better the higher it rises.

(3) The verse encourages repeated acts of charity, since good character traits will not become firm and stable in the soul unless they are done repeatedly. This is a very important point.

(4) One notable allusion found in this verse is that sincere charity has one benefit which is immediate and another which is deferred. The immediate benefit is that the characteristics of charitableness

---

9: Ibn 'Ajība, *Tafsīr*, commentary on Qur'ān 2:265, paraphrasing Ibn 'Aṭā' Allāh, *Ḥikam*, Aphorism no. 45.

حساً قبلها الله منهم وجعلها كثيرة معنى وذلك لأنها نابعة من نفوس ارتاضت على البذل وحاولت الفضائل حتى صارت المعالى لها ديدنا. فإنفاق المال بإخلاص من أعظم ما ترسُخُ به الطاعة في النفس لأنه تنقية لها من الشُّح والتعلق.

ومِن جماليات هذا المثل وبلاغته:

(١) مواساةُ أهل الإخلاص إذ لا تخلوا أعمالهم عن فائدة لصحة أساسها وملاحة أصلها، فصحة الأصل منبع كل خير ومع ذلك فالآيات تُحفّز على الترقي والزيادة، كي تنمو ثمرات الأعمال وتتضاعف نتائجها وكما قال بعض العارفين: تنمية الأعمال على قدر تصفية الأحوال، وتصفية الأحوال على قدر التحقق بمقامات الإنزال (أي مقامات اليقين). فكلّ مَن تحقق بالنزول في مقامات اليقين فكُلُّ أعمالِه عظيمة.

(٢) تشبيه النفس الفاضلة الكريمة بالجنةِ وتشبيه تسنمها مقام الإخلاص بالربوة وفي هذا المقام كل ما يخرج منها حسن، إن لم يكن بأثر وابل، فطلّ. وهو مظهر بهيج يزيد حسن الجنة حسنا فكلما علت طاب ثمرها.

(٣) أنَّ في الآيةِ تحريضاً على تَكْرَارِ الإِنفَاقِ إذْ إن ثباتَ الأَخْلاقِ ورُسُوخِهَا في النَّفسِ لا يَتَأَتَّى إلا بتكرارها وهو معنى جليل.

(٤) في الآية ملمح جميل وهو أن فائدة النفقة للمخلص فائدة عاجلة وهي تمكن أخلاق البذل والإنفاق نم النفس

and generosity become more and more entrenched in the soul until they become second nature; the deferred benefit is the reward of the Hereafter. That is perhaps what the twofold yield symbolizes. At the very least, the sincere giver earns the reward and good pleasure of God, which is good in any case.

حتى تصير طبعا، وأخرى آجلة وهي الثواب وكأن هذا يقابل الضعفين. وعلى أقل الأحوال، فالمخلص يتعرض لثواب الله ورضوانه فهو بخير على كل حال.

Parable 4: The Biting Wind

Sūrat Āl 'Imrān (3), Verse 117

The likeness of what they spend in the present life is as that of a biting wind that smites the field of a people who have wronged themselves, and destroys it. God wronged them not, but they do wrong themselves.

This parable depicts the charity of the unbelievers and the dire consequences which it brings upon them. Using a tangible concept to represent an intelligible one, it compares their charity, which is annulled by their unbelief in God and retains no value, to a field which is struck by a cold wind that destroys it and leaves its owner utterly ruined,.

One could describe this simile as a composite of several similes combined together. God compares their spending on good causes to a cold wind bereft of warmth because of how those deeds, and indeed all their deeds, are bereft of the warmth of faith. The cold wind spoils the crops, while a good wind would have carried goodness and pollen from one plant to another. And since their deeds and expenditures were devoid of faith, they were cold and harmful, bringing nothing but ruin, with no life in them, just as a body becomes cold when the spirit leaves it.

One could also say that the parable compares the ruination of their charitable spending and the annulment of their reward to the destruction caused by a biting wind, a wind that howls and chills. Their donations and deeds end up as ruined and destroyed as a field

المثل الرابع: ريحٌ صرصر
سورةُ آلِ عمران الآية: (١١٧)

﴿ مَثَلُ مَا يُنْفِقُونَ فِي هَذِهِ الْحَيَاةِ الدُّنْيَا كَمَثَلِ رِيحٍ فِيهَا صِرٌّ أَصَابَتْ حَرْثَ قَوْمٍ ظَلَمُوا أَنْفُسَهُمْ فَأَهْلَكَتْهُ وَمَا ظَلَمَهُمُ اللَّهُ وَلَكِنْ أَنْفُسَهُمْ يَظْلِمُونَ ﴾

هذا المثلُ يُضربُ لنفَقاتِ الكُفَّارِ، وما تعود به مِن بوارٍ وخيبة على أصحابها. فهو يشبه إنفاقهم الذي يُحبطهُ كُفرهم بالله فلا يبقي له أثرا، بهيئةِ زرعٍ أصابته ريحٌ باردةٌ فأهلكته وتركت أصحَابهُ في حسرةٍ شديدةٍ، فهو تشبيهٌ للمعقولِ بالمَحْسُوس.

وَقدْ يُقالُ إنَّ هذا التشبيهَ مُركَّبٌ من تشبيهاتٍ أُدْمِجَ بعضُها في بعضٍ، فنقول: إنه شبّهَ نَفَقَتَهُم في أعمالِ الخيرِ بالريح الباردةِ الخَاليةِ عن الدفء، وذلك لخلوها - بل وخلوِّ أعمالِهِم كُلِّها- عن حرارةِ الإيمان. والريحُ الباردة تفسدُ الزرع بينما الريحُ الطيبة تحملُ الخير والطلعَ من نبته لأخرى، فلما خلت أعمالهم ونفقاتهم عن الإيمان صارت باردةً ضارةً لا أثر لها إلا الهلاك، لا حياة فيها كالميت إذا خرجتْ منه الروح يبرُد.

ويُمكِنُ أن نقول أيضا إنه مثَّلَ إتلاف النفقات

that has been struck by a wind and turned into a barren plain.

Other notable features of this parable include:

(1) It shows that if one does not achieve true sincerity, his actions will be deficient in some way, and they will be so empty and weak that even the slightest wind will uproot them and topple them.

(2) The reason the parable mentions a field specifically is that it is a place where effort is necessary and where long work bears fruit, just as wealth or property necessitates effort and is the fruit of action. The anguish caused by the destruction of the field resembles in several respects the anguish felt when expenditures are wasted. Firstly, a field needs effort, and so does charitable giving. Secondly, a field cannot dispense with outlay in the form of planting, watering, and preparation; similarly, an unbeliever who gives charity will not fail, given the way he is, to seek to improve his image in the eyes of other people.

(3) If we say that a biting (*ṣarṣar*) wind means one which howls (*taṣirr*), this adds further depth to the parable. Someone who gives charity proudly always raises his voice to speak about it, whether literally or figuratively. The consequence of this is that a howling wind will come along and disturb his voice, overwhelming his pride. Or if we say that *ṣarṣar* means 'very cold', this is an allusion to the deadness and coldness of their hearts, for no faith dwells in them.

وإبطالَ ثوابها بهيئةِ إتلاف ريح لها صرٌّ- والصرُّ هو الصوت والبرد. والمُرادُ تشبيه النفقةِ والأعمال - في تلفها وضياعها- بحرثٍ ضربته ريح فأصبح صعيداً زَلَقَا.

ومِنْ لطائفِ هذا المثل:

(١) أنه أشار إلى أن كلَّ مَنْ لم يتَحقق بالإخلاص لا تَخلو أعماله مِن عِلَلٍ، فأعْمَالهُ فارِغَةٌ ضعيفةٌ أَقَلُّ ريحٍ تقتلعها وتُسقطها.

(٢) أنّه خصَّ الحرث لأنه موضعُ الجهدِ وثمرةَ العملِ الطويلِ كما أنَّ الأموال محلُّ الجهد وثمرةُ السعي. فالحسرةُ بهلاك الزرع تشبه الحسرة بضياع النفقات وبوارها من جهاتٍ، أولها: أن الحرث موضع جهد وكذلك النفقة، وثانيها: أن الحرث لا يخلو عن نفقة بذر وسقاية وإعداد، وكذلك المُنفقُ من أهل الكفر لا يخلو حاله عن طلب تسوية صورته في أعين الناس.

(٣) إن قلنا أن الريح الصرصر هي التي تصرّ أي تصوت كان في التشبيه معنى عميق وهو أن المُفاخِرَ بنَفَقَتِه يرفع بها صوته متحدثا عنها (حسا أو معنى) فكانت عقوبته ريح فيها صوت يشوش على صوته ويغطي على تَفاخُرِه. وإن قلنا إن الصرصرَ هو البرد الشديد، كان إشارةً لموتِ قلوبهم وبرودتها لأن الإيمان لا يَسْكُنُها.

Parable 5: The Orphan's Property Brings Terrible Torment

Sūrat al-Nisā' (4), Verse 10

Truly those who consume the property of orphans unjustly are consuming fire in their bellies, no less; and they shall enter a blaze.

In this parable the orphan's property, when consumed unjustly, is compared to fire that burns and destroys all that it touches. That is because anyone who usurps the orphan's property does so in order to seek benefit and profit for himself.

Therefore, the verse compares wealth, which is taken in that manner to fire, and likens its usurper to someone who consumes fire which disfigures his physiognomy, burns his innards, and destroys him both inwardly and outwardly.

The choice of the word "fire" in this parable is certainly made for a very precise reason. If any other consumable thing had been chosen, someone might argue that it might contain some kind of nourishing value which could justify the pain endured upon consuming it. Consider how people may eat foul-smelling foods because they taste pleasant, or consume substances which both smell and taste foul because they provide some sort of medical benefit. But there is no benefit whatsoever to eating fire, but only burning, pain, disfigurement, and regret.

Other subtle lessons of this parable include:

المثل الخامس: مالُ اليتيم عذابٌ أليم
سورةُ النساء الآية (١٠)

﴿إِنَّ الَّذِينَ يَأْكُلُونَ أَمْوَالَ الْيَتَامَى ظُلْمًا إِنَّمَا يَأْكُلُونَ فِي بُطُونِهِمْ نَارًا وَسَيَصْلَوْنَ سَعِيرًا﴾

في هذا المثل، شبّه مالَ اليتيم الذي يُؤكَلُ ظلما بالنّارِ التي تأتي على الأخضرِ واليابسِ وتَحْرِقُ ما يعتَرِضُها وتُفسِدُهُ. وذلك لأنَّ آكِلَ مالِ اليتيمِ يفعلُ ذلكَ طَلباً للنفعِ والاستفادةِ لِنفسهِ فشبهتِ الآياتِ ذلك المال في تلك الحال بالنّارِ وجَعلَت آكلهُ كأنهُ يأْكُلُ ناراً تحرِقُ أَحشاءه وتُدَمِّرُ باطِنَهُ وظاهِرَهُ وتُشَوّه خِلْقَتَهُ.

ولاشكَّ أن اختيار "النار" في هذا المثلِ اختيارٌ دقيقٌ جداً إذ لو اختيرَ شيء من المطعوماتِ مع الأُكلِ، قد يقول قائلهم: لعلَّ ثمة غذاءٍ في هذا المطعوم يُتَحمّلُ أذاه من أجله ألا ترى بعضهم يَستسيغُ المطعومَ قَبيحَ الرِّيحِ لحلاوةِ طعمِهِ أوْ قبيحَ الريحِ والطَّعمِ لفائدةٍ صحيةٍ قَد تَحصُلَ لآكله. أما النارُ، فأي فائدةٍ في أَكلِهَا سوى الحرق والألم والتشوهِ والنَّدَم.

(1) It alludes to the consequences awaiting all who usurp the property of orphans in the Hereafter, of which they will be informed on the Day of Resurrection. Al-Suddī[10] said, "When a man consumes an orphan's property unlawfully, he will be brought forth on the Day of Resurrection with flames of fire issuing forth from his mouth, ears, and eyes. All who see him will know that he usurped an orphan's property."

(2) This penalty is more severe than that suffered for refusing to render zakat, for two reasons. Firstly, the pauper who receives zakat does not own the part of the *niṣāb* which is given to him before it is rendered to him, and so denying it to him is not denying him his own property.

On the other hand, the orphan is the rightful owner of the usurped property, and so denying it to him is denying him what is rightfully his, which is worse.

Secondly, the pauper might be an adult who is able to earn a living in some other way, which the orphan cannot do because he or she is only a child. Because of the severity of this penalty, when this verse was revealed the Companions stopped associating with orphans altogether, and so the Qur'ān commanded them to associate with them, saying: *If you mingle with them, they are your brothers. God knows one who works corruption from one who sets things right* [Qur'ān 2:220].

(3) The specifying of a punishment of fire might have another reason, namely that the usurper of the orphan's property ruins his future prospects and causes him psychological suffering, and both of these effects apply with fire. That is why He uses metaphor rather than simile: in other words, He does not say, 'it is as though they are consuming fire', but rather says, *[they] are consuming fire, no less.*

(4) The parable speaks of "consuming" in particular for several

10: Ismā'īl al-Suddī (d. c. 127/745) was a scholar and preacher of Kufa.

وفي المثل لطائف خفية منها:

(١) أنَّه إشاره إلى عقوبة آكلِ مالِ اليتيم في الآخرةِ التي يُعرَفُ بها يوم القيامة. قال السُّدي: إذا أكَلَ الرجلُ مال اليتيم ظُلماً يُبعَثُ يوم القيامةِ ولهبُ النَارِ يخرُجُ مِنْ فيهِ وَمَسَامعه وأُذُنَيهِ وعينيه، يَعرِفُ كلُّ من رآه أنه أكل مالَ اليتيم.

(٢) أن هذه العقوبة أشدّ من عقوبةِ منعِ الزكاةِ من وجهين، الأول: أن الفقير الذي يتلقى الزكاه لا يملكُ جزءَ النصابِ الذي يُعطى له قبل أن يُدفَع له فمنعهُ منه ليس منعاً له من ماله هو بينما اليتيم مالكٌ لذلك المالِ المَأكول ظلماً، فمنعه منه منعٌ له من ملكه وهو أقبح. والثاني: أن الفقير قد يكون كبيرا قادرا على الاكتساب من طرق أخرى واليتيم عاجز لصغره وضعفه. ومِن أجل شدّة العقوبة هذه، امتنع الصحابة عن مُخالطةِ اليتامى بالكلية لما نزلت هذه الآيةِ فأمرهم القرآن بالمخالطة في قوله تعالى: **وإنْ تُخَالِطوهم فإخوانكم والله يَعْلَمُ المُفْسِدَ مِن المُصْلِحِ**. (البقرة: ٢٢٠)

(٣) لعلَّ التخصيص بعقوبة النار أيضا سببه أن آكلَ مالِ اليتيمِ يُتْلِف مستقبله ويُحْدثُ له ألَماً نفسياً. والنارُ تشتملُ على المعنَيينِ ولذا عدل عن التشبيه إلى الاستعارةِ فلم يَقُلْ: يَأكلونَ أموَالاً كالنّارِ، بلْ قالَ: يأْكُلُونَ ناراً.

(٤) تَخْصيصُ الأَكْلِ لوجوهٍ منها: [١] أن العادة جرت فيمن أنفق ماله في وجوه مراداته أن يقال "أكل ماله" [٢] وأن

reasons, including the following: [i] it is customary to speak of someone who spends his wealth on the things he desires as "consuming his wealth"; [ii] most wealth is spent upon consumption; and [iii] most wealth in those days was held in the form of livestock, whose meat was eaten and whose milk was drunk.

الأكل هو المُعظَم [٣] وأنَّ الأَموالَ في ذلك الوَقت كانت عَامَّتُها أنعاماً تؤكَلُ لحومها وتُشربُ ألبانُها.

Parable 6: The Muḥammadan Light

Sūrat al-Mā'ida (5), Verse 15

There has come to you from God a light and a manifest Book.

This verse contains a similitude, as many scholars have affirmed, in which the Prophet ﷺ is likened to light. That is because sensory light gives the outer vision the power to perceive things, while supra-sensory light gives the inner vision the power to perceive realities and intelligibles. Likewise, the Prophet ﷺ guides us outwardly toward teachings, laws, and outward ethical traits, and inwardly toward faith and inward ethical traits. He teaches outwardly and instructs inwardly. By means of him our outer beings are set right, and through love for him our interiors and inner visions are made upright.

Descriptions of the Prophet ﷺ inform us of his outward light, saying that he was "luminous when uncovered" (*anwar al-mutajarrid*), meaning that his body was luminous. It was also related by Anas ibn Mālik ؓ that when Abū Bakr al-Ṣiddīq ؓ saw him approaching, he recited this line of verse:

> The Trusted Chosen One who calls to goodness,
> Like the full moon shining through the darkness!

Umm Ma'bad al-Khuzā'iyya described him ﷺ as being radiant in appearance, and said that his neck shone. The poet Ka'b ibn

المثل السادس: النور المحمدي
سورةُ المائدة الآية (١٥)

﴿قَدْ جَاءَكُمْ مِنَ اللهِ نُورٌ وَكِتَابٌ مُبِينٌ﴾

تحتوي هذه الآية على تشبيهٍ - كما قال كثيرٌ من العلماء- وهو تشبيهه صلى الله عليه وسلم بالنورِ. وذلكَ لأن النور الحسي يتقوى به البصرُ على إدراكِ الأشياء والنور المعنوي تتقوى به البصائر على إدراك الحقائق والمعقولات. وكذلك هو صلوات الله وسلامه عليه - يهدي في الظاهر إلى المعالم والأحكام والأخلاق الظاهرة وفي الباطن إلى الإيمان والأخلاق الباطنة، يُعَلّمُ ظاهرا ويُلَقِّنُ باطنا وبه تنصلح الظواهر وبمحبته تستقيم البواطن والبصائر.

وقَدْ وردَ في وصفه ﷺ مما يدلُّ على نوره الظاهر أنّه كان "أنورَ المُتجرد" أي نيّرَ الجسم. ومنه أيضا أن أنس بن مالك رضي الله عنه روى أن أبا بكر الصديق رضي الله عنه كان إذا رآه ﷺ مقبلا قال:

أمين مصطفى بالخير يدعو، كضوء البدر زايله الظلام

وفي وصف أم معبد الخزاعية له ﷺ أنه كان ظاهر الوضاءة وأن في عنقه سطَع (أي نور وضياء) ولذلك مدحه كعب بن

Zuhayr ﷺ described him by saying:

> The Messenger is truly a light which gives radiance,
> An Indian blade, an unsheathed Sword of God!

The exalted meanings contained in this parable include:

(1) Light was chosen because of its inherent constancy. Whenever people want to compare anything, they compare it to light, and experts tell us that there is nothing in the universe whose speed is constant and fixed except for light, which travels through space without it depending on color or density.

(2) It is certain that bodies require light and that eyes require light, and life cannot exist without it. The same is true of the Prophet ﷺ, for there can be no life without connecting to him and receiving from him. The great imam and Knower of God Shaykh al-Islam ʿAlī ibn Muḥammad ibn Ḥusayn al-Ḥabashī al-Ḥusaynī (d. 1333/1915) says in his *dīwān* of poetry entitled *al-Jawhar al-maknūn wal-sirr al-maṣūn* ("The Hidden Jewel and the Well-Guarded Secret"):

> He is the light whose radiance guides the perplexed;
> At the Gathering, his Banner will shade God's Envoys.
> He received wisdom purely from the Unseen,
> Which his sky rained down over the East and West.
> The People of Truth witnessed graces from him,
> Showing that glory and ultimate splendor are his.
> By God, there is no sight the eye could behold
> That is dearer than him to those veiled from him.

زهير رضي الله عنه في محضره فقال:

إن الرسول لنور يستضاء به، مهندٌ من سيوف الله مسلول

ومن المعاني الرائقة التي يشملها هذا المثل:

(١) أن اختيار النور لثبات حقيقته حتى أنهم إذا قاسوا شيئا قاسوه بسرعة الضوء. وفي ذلك يؤكد المختصون أنه ليس في الكون سرعة مقررة ثابتة إلا سرعة النور وهي في الفضاء لا تعتمد على لون ولا كثافة.

(٢) أن حاجة الأجسام للنور متحققة وحاجة الأبصار إليه متحققة أيضا فلا تكون الحياة بدونه وهو كذلك صلوات الله وسلامه عليه لا حياة بدون الاتصال به والتلقي عنه. يقول الإمام شيخ الإسلام العارف بالله تعالى علي بن محمد بن حسين الحبشي الحسيني (١٢٥٩ - ١٣٣٣هـ) في ديوانه الفاخر المسمى الجوهر المكنون والسرِّ المصون:

هُوَ النُّورُ يَهْدِي الحَائِرِينَ ضِيَاؤُهُ
وَفِي الحَشْرِ ظِلُّ المُرسَلِين لِوَاؤُه.
تَلَقَّي مِن الغَيْبِ المُجَرَّدِ حِكْمَةً
بِهَا أَمْطَرَتْ فِي الخَافِقَيْنِ سَمَاؤُه.
ومَشْـهُودُ أهلِ الحقِّ مِنْهُ لَطَائِفٌ
تُخَبِّرُ أَنَّ المجـدَ والشَأوَ شَـأوُه.
فَلِلَّهِ مَا لِلْعَينِ مِنْ مَشْهَدِ اجتِلا
يَعِزُّ على أَهْلِ الحِجَابِ اجتِلاؤُه.

Parable 7: The Victims of Delusion

Sūrat al-An'ām (6), Verse 71

Say: Shall we call upon that which neither profits us nor hurts us, instead of God, and so be turned back on our heels after God has guided us? Like one whom devils have led astray in the earth, bewildered, while his companions call him to guidance, "Come to us!" Say: Truly God's guidance is the only guidance, and we have been commanded to submit to the Lord of the Worlds.

This parable depicts the state of those who renege from Islam and faith and turn back to idolatry, unbelief, and error, abandoning their Muslim companions. It compares them to someone who loses his mind and wanders in the land whose roads he previously knew, as though demons have taken control of him and led him astray from the right path, stealing away his mind, even while his companions call him to come back to the road as he drifts off away from them.

The Arabs believed that when a person lost his sanity, the jinn had stolen his mind and sent him in whatever direction they desired. They used to say of such a person that the devils had led him astray, or the jinn had captured him. One of the best-known stories about this is the account of 'Amr ibn 'Adī al-Lakhmī, the nephew of the King of Ḥīra Judhayma ibn Mālik. This curious parable, then, was based upon the prevalent beliefs of those to whom it was addressed, in order to make the point clearer to them.

The purpose of this parable was to make certain idolaters give up

المثلُ السَّابِعُ: ضحايا الأوهام
سُورَةُ الأنعامِ الآيةُ (٧١)

﴿ قُلْ أَنَدْعُو مِنْ دُونِ اللَّهِ مَا لَا يَنْفَعُنَا وَلَا يَضُرُّنَا وَنُرَدُّ عَلَى أَعْقَابِنَا بَعْدَ إِذْ هَدَانَا اللَّهُ كَالَّذِي اسْتَهْوَتْهُ الشَّيَاطِينُ فِي الْأَرْضِ حَيْرَانَ لَهُ أَصْحَابٌ يَدْعُونَهُ إِلَى الْهُدَى ائْتِنَا قُلْ إِنَّ هُدَى اللَّهِ هُوَ الْهُدَى وَأُمِرْنَا لِنُسْلِمَ لِرَبِّ الْعَالَمِينَ ﴾

هذا المثل تشبيهٌ لحالِ مَنْ يرجعُ من الإسلام والإيمان إلى الشركِ والكُفرِ والضلالةِ ويترُكُ أصحابَهُ من المسلمين بحالِ من فَسَدَ عقله فتاه في الأرضِ بعد أن كان عاقلاً عارِفاً بِمَسالِكِها وكَأَنَّ الشياطينَ قد تمَلَّكتهُ فأضلَّتهُ عن الجادّةِ وذهبت بعقله مع وجودِ أصحابٍ له يدعونه لسلوك الجادّةِ وهو هائم عنهم.

وكانت العرب تعتقدُ فيمن أصابه مسٌّ ذهبَ بعقله أنَّ الجِنَّ قد اختَطَفتْ عقله فسيّرَتهُ كما تريدُ وكانوا يقولون عن أمثالِ هؤلاء: استهوته الشياطين واختطفته الجنُّ. ومِنْ أشهرِ مَنْ أُطْلِقَ عليهم هذا عمرو بن عديّ اللخمي ابن أختِ جُذَيمَةَ بن مالكٍ ملكِ الحيرةِ. فَبُنِيَ هذا التمثيل العجيبُ على اعتقاد المخاطبين كي يُؤَكِّد المعنى لديهم تأكيدا.

hope of their Muslim relatives ever leaving the religion. It is related that Sa'īd ibn Zayd, the husband of 'Umar ibn al-Khaṭṭāb's sister, was treated very harshly by 'Umar [before 'Umar's own conversion] due to his having embraced Islam. Likewise, it is related that 'Abd al-Raḥmān the son of Abū Bakr used to call his father to return to idol-worship. There are many well-known accounts of pagan parents threatening their children who had converted to Islam, which can be found in the works of Prophetic biography. For example, the mother of Muṣ'ab ibn 'Umayr ﷺ, whose name was Khunās bint Mālik, threatened him and locked him up. Sa'd ibn Abī Waqqāṣ ﷺ was likewise threatened and rebuked by his own mother, who denied him food and drink. Walīd ibn al-Walīd ibn al-Mughīra, the brother of Khālid ibn al-Walīd, was also locked up due to his conversion, and there were many others.

The verse contains several other lessons, including these:

(1) The verse features an independent clause followed by the phrase *and so be turned back on our heels*, a common expression indicating the state of one who returns to an unpleasant situation after having left it. If someone sets out to perform a task or fulfil some objective but then returns before he has done what he set out to do, it is as if he has turned back on his heels, meaning that he has wasted his effort, it being inconceivable to view any intelligent person turning back on his heels in a positive light.

(2) The parable contains a wonderfully ingenious composite which may be deconstructed as follows: unbelief is represented by bewilderment, apostasy by insanity, idolaters by devils, and the call to faith by companions who call people to guidance.

(3) The parable suggests that the fruits of faith include equilibrium, composure, sanity, and protection from devils and their helpers, as well as clear orientation. The unbeliever, in contrast, wanders directionlessly and aimlessly, bereft of dignity and protection. This

والغرضُ من هذا التمثيل تأييسُ بعض المشركين من ارتداد أقاربهم من المُسلمين عن الدين فقد ورد في الخبر أنَّ سعيدَ بن زيد زوجُ أختِ عمرَ بنِ الخطابِ لقيَ من عمر شدة وغلظة بسبب إسلامه. كما وردَ أنَّ عبد الرحمن بن أبي بكر كانَ يدعو أباهُ لِعبادةِ الأصنامِ. وَخَبرُ تهديدِ كثيرٍ من الآباءِ والأُمّهاتِ أبناءَهُم ممن أسلَمُوا مشهورٌ وقصصهم مبثوثة في كتب السيرةِ منهم مصعبُ بن عمير (رضي الله عنه) هددته أمه خُناس بنت مالك وحبسته، وسعدُ بن أبي وقّاص (رضي الله عنه) هددته أمه ووبخته وامتنعت عن الطعام والشراب، ومنهم الوليد بن الوليد بن المُغيرة أخو خالد بن الوليد حُبس بسبب إسلامه وغيرهم كثيرون.

وفي الآية فضلا عما سبق لطائف منها:

(١) الآية فيها استئنافٌ ابتدائي بعده جملةُ "**ونردُّ على أَعْقابنا**" وهو تعبير شائعٌ يصور حال من تلبس بحالةٍ ذميمةٍ بعد أَن فارَقها. وذلك أن الخارجَ لقضاء أمرٍ أو تحصيل غرض يريده إن عادَ قبلِ إتمام غرضه وبلوغِ قصده، كانَ كالرَّاجع على عقبيه أي كَمَنْ أضاع جُهْدَهُ إذ لا يُتَصَوّر في عاقلٍ أن يعود على عقبيه ويكون في هذا خيرٌ أبداً.

(٢) في التشبيه تركيبٌ بديع يصلُحُ للتفكيكِ؛ فالكُفْرُ كالهُيام، والارتِدَادُ ذِهَابُ العَقْلِ، والمُشركُون كالشياطين، والدعوة للإيمان أصحابٌ يدعونه إلى الهُدى.

(٣) كَأنَّ التشبيه يُشيرُ إلى أنَّ من ثمراتِ الإيمان الاتزانُ

idea is further emphasized elsewhere in the sura, where God Most High tells us of how Abraham the Close Friend [of God] said, *Truly I have turned my face to Him Who originated the heavens and the earth, as a man of pure faith; and I am not of the idolaters* [Qur'ān 6:79], and again at the end of the sura when He says, *Say, Truly my prayer and my rituals, and my living and my dying, are for God, the Lord of the Worlds* [Qur'ān 6:162].

والرصانةُ والعقل والحصانه من الشياطين وأعوانهم فضلا عن وضوح الوجهة، أما صاحبُ الكفرِ فهو يتقلبُ بلا وجهة ولا غايةٍ لا حرمةَ له ولا حصانةً. ويتأكدُ هذا المعنى في السورة في قوله تعالى على لسانِ إبراهيمَ الخليل: "**إِنِّي وَجَّهْتُ وَجْهِيَ لِلَّذِي فَطَرَ السَّمَاوَاتِ وَالْأَرْضَ حَنِيفًا وَمَا أَنَا مِنَ الْمُشْرِكِينَ**" (الأنعام: ٧٩) وفي آخر السورة في قوله تعالى: **قُلْ إِنَّ صَلَاتِي وَنُسُكِي وَمَحْيَايَ وَمَمَاتِي لِلهِ رَبِّ الْعَالَمِينَ** (الأنعام: ١٦٢)

Parable 8: Between Life and Death

Sūrat al-Anʿām (6), Verse 122

Is he who was dead and to whom We then gave life and appointed for him a light by which to walk among people, like him who is in darknesses from which he cannot emerge? So it is that the deeds of the disbelievers are made to seem appealing to them.

This is an ingenious similitude composed of several parts, comparing the state of someone who moves from unbelief to faith, and from error to guidance, to a dead person who lies bereft of all means of goodness and benefit until life is poured upon him and he rises, brushing the dust from himself, and is then provided with a light by which he may differentiate between things and recognize the truth, so that when falsehood approaches him, he may avoid it.

Without doubt, idolatry is a barrier which prevents differentiation between truth and falsehood, because it diverts a person away from the quest for that in which his welfare and salvation in the Hereafter lie. He stands amid multiple darknesses, so that even if he escaped from one he would be shrouded by another. But when God guides him to Islam, his state is entirely transformed, and he becomes able to differentiate between the beneficial and the harmful and to pursue what is good for him and steer clear of the path of corruption. It is as though he is bathed in light, walking amid people. Consider how in his original state he was like nothing so much as a corpse, but in the state of faith he has become truly and completely

المَثلُ الثامِن: بين الحياة والموت
سورة الأنعامِ الآية (١٢٢)

﴿ أَوَمَنْ كَانَ مَيْتًا فَأَحْيَيْنَاهُ وَجَعَلْنَا لَهُ نُورًا يَمْشِي بِهِ فِي النَّاسِ كَمَنْ مَثَلُهُ فِي الظُّلُمَاتِ لَيْسَ بِخَارِجٍ مِنْهَا كَذَٰلِكَ زُيِّنَ لِلْكَافِرِينَ مَا كَانُوا يَعْمَلُونَ ﴾

هذا تشبيهٌ بديعٌ يتركبُ من أجزاء حيث شبّه هيئةَ مَن ينتقلُ من الكفرِ إلى الإيمانِ، ومن الضلالة إلى الهداية بميَتٍ فقد جميع أسباب الخير والفائدة صُبَّت عليه الحياةُ صباً فانبعث ينفضُ عن نفسه التراب، ثمَّ مُنحَ نوراً يُمَيِّزُ به الأشياء ويعرفُ به وجه الحقِّ فَيَأتيهِ والبَاطِلِ فيُجَافِيهِ.

ولاشكَّ أن الشركَ يحولُ دون التمييز بين الحقِّ والباطِلِ لأنه يصرِفُ صاحِبَهُ عن السعي إلى ما فيه صلاحُ معادِهِ ونجاته في آخرَتِهِ وهو في ظُلُماتٍ لو أفاق من واحدةٍ لاكْتَنَفَتْهُ أُخرى، فإذا هداهُ الله إلى الإسلامِ تَغيّرَ حالُهُ بالكلية فصارَ يُميّزُ بين الصالح والفاسد ويسعى لما فيه الصلاح ويتنكب سبيل الفساد فكأنّهُ في نور يمشي بين الناسِ. ألا تراه إذاً في حالته الأولى أشبه ما يكون بالميّتِ بينما هو في حال الإيمان حيٌّ حياةً تامةً. فانتقاله من الحالة الأولى للثانية

alive. His transformation from the first state to the second is like being resurrected after death. The allegorical elements of the parable are as follows: the unbeliever is represented by the dead man, the believer by the living man, and guidance by resurrection.

The beautiful rhetorical features of this parable include:

(1) It features a contrast between qualities whose goodness is illustrated by their opposites. God makes contrasts between death, life, light, and darkness, and then attributes the gift of life to Himself, saying, *and then We gave him life*. This is a tremendous honor, for it implies that He performed the revivification personally, which evokes the immensity of the grace and favor.

(2) It is said that He compares unbelief to death because it is ignorance, and ignorance leads to confusion and immobility, which in turn resembles death, which causes stillness. A dead person cannot be guided to anything, and nor can an ignorant person. One might object that we see many people who do not believe in God, yet who possess minds that are intelligent and sharp. How can that be?

The answer is that what is meant here is a human being's knowledge of the purpose of his creation, the secret wisdom behind his existence, and the reality of his being a vicegerent of God. If he is oblivious to that, he is ignorant—no matter how much exoteric empirical knowledge he may have acquired.

God the Exalted says of such people, *They know an outward aspect of the present life, but of the Hereafter they are oblivious* [Qur'ān 30:7], affirming that they possess knowledge which is limited, outward, and firmly attached to this present life.

He says elsewhere, *So shun him who turns away from Our Remembrance and desires nothing but the present life. That is the full extent of their knowledge* [Qur'ān 53:29-30], affirming that they have knowledge which has an extent and a limit that is restricted to this ephemeral life. The people of true realization do not consider that to be knowledge at all. Real knowledge is that which spreads rays of light

كالبعث بعد الموت. وأَجْزَاءُ التَّشْبِيهِ هي: الكافر مشبّهٌ بالميت والمؤمنُ مشبّهٌ بالحي والهدايةُ تشبَه بالبعثِ.

ومِن بلاغةِ هذا التشبيهِ وجماله:

(١) أنّهُ طَابقَ بين أوصافٍ يَظهَرُ جمالها بضدها؛ فقد طابق بين الموت والحياة والنور والظلمات ثم نسب الحياة لنفسه فقال: "**فأحييناه**" وهذا تشريف عظيم إذ كأنه سبحانه باشر الإحياء بنفسه فهو إشعارٌ بعظيم المنّةِ والفضل.

(٢) قيل إنه جعل الكفر موتا لأنه جهل والجهل يوجب الحيرةَ والوقفة فهو كالموتِ الذي يوجِبُ السكونَ. والميتُ لا يهتدي لشيء وكذا الجاهل. وقد يعترض البعض فيقول: إننا نرى كثيرا ممن لا يؤمنون بالله تعالى من أصحاب العقولِ الذكية الألمعية فكيف يكون هذا؟ وجواب المعترضِ أن المقصود هنا معرفةُ الإنسان بغاية خلقه وسرِّ وجوده وحقيقةِ خلافَتِهِ عن الله، فإن غاب عنه ذلك صار جاهلا وإن بلغ من العلم التجريبي الظاهرِ ما بلغ. وقد قال الله في أمثال هذا: "**يَعْلَمُونَ ظَاهِرًا مِنَ الْحَيَاةِ الدُّنْيَا وَهُمْ عَنِ الْآخِرَةِ هُمْ غَافِلُونَ**" (الروم: ٧) فأثبت لهم علما ظاهرا محدودا متعلقا بهذه الحياة الدنيا. وقال في موضع آخر: " **فَأَعْرِضْ عَنْ مَنْ تَوَلَّى عَنْ ذِكْرِنَا وَلَمْ يُرِدْ إِلَّا الْحَيَاةَ الدُّنْيَا * ذَلِكَ مَبْلَغُهُمْ مِنَ الْعِلْمِ**"(النّجم: ٢٩-٣٠) فأثبت لهم علماً له مبلغٌ ونهايةٌ مرتبطةٌ بهذه الحياة الفانيةِ وهذا ليس علما عند أهل التحقيق، فالعلم ما انبسط في الصدر شعاعه وينكشف عن القلب قناعه. ولمثل هذا المعنى أشار الإمام السيد عبد الرحمن بن عبد الله بلفقيه في

through the breast and lifts the veil from the heart. Imam Sayyid ʿAbd al-Raḥmān ibn ʿAbd Allāh Balfaqīh alludes to this in his poem *Rashafāt ahl al-kamāl*, saying:

> A man may be learned in every science,
> But if he has not tasted them he's heedless, asleep.
> His state's as fearful as that of the bewildered
> When he comes face to face with death and its horrors.

منظومته المسماة بالرشفات:

وَمَنْ يَكُنْ بِكُلِّ عِلْمٍ عَالِمُ
وَلَمْ يَذُقْهَا فَهُوَ سَاهٍ نَائِـــمُ
فَخِفْ عَلَيْهِ مَا يَخَافُ الهَائِمُ
عِنْدَ كَفَاحِ المَوْتِ والأَهْوَالِ

Parable 9: The Expansion of Faith

Sūrat al-Anʿām (6), Verse 125

When God desires to guide someone, He opens his breast to Islam.

In this parable, God the Glorious and Exalted depicts the revealing of reality to the heart and the unveiling of the truth of Islam to the soul so that it feels at peace with it and accepts it. He likens this to cutting open meat and uncovering what lies beneath it so that nothing remains hidden. The point of comparison between the two is the attainment of realization and clarity, which brings peace of mind and dispels all uncertainty.

The word *sharḥ* (to open, incise, expand, or explain) can be used literally to mean cutting flesh or meat, and figuratively to mean revealing and clarifying something. The latter would mean that God Most High places, in the minds of those He wishes to guide, a certain aptitude, preparedness, and receptivity toward Islam so that they incline toward it and feel well-disposed to it. That is how it resembles *sharḥ* in the sense of opening something to view what is beneath it, so that no doubt or uncertainty remains.

Al-Ṭabarānī and others narrate on the authority of Ibn Masʿūd that some people asked, "Messenger of God, how does God open someone's heart to Islam?" The Messenger of God replied, "He casts light into it so that it expands." They asked, "Is there any sign to tell that this has happened?" He replied, "Turning toward the abode of eternity, shunning the abode of delusion, and preparing for death

المثلُ التاسع: سعةُ الإيمان
سورة الأنعام الآية (١٢٥)

﴿ فَمَنْ يُرِدِ اللَّهُ أَنْ يَهْدِيَهُ يَشْرَحْ صَدْرَهُ لِلْإِسْلَامِ ﴾

في هذا المثلِ، شبَّه الحقُّ سبحانهُ وتعالى انْجِلاءَ الحقيقةِ للقلبِ وانكشافَ صدقِ الإسلامِ للنفس حتى إنها تسكن إليه وتُقبلُ عليه بشَقِّ اللحمِ وانكشافِ ما دونهُ حتى لم يعُد ثَمّةَ خفاءٍ. ووجهُ المشابهة بين الأمرين حصول التحقق والبيان الذي يترتب عليه سكون البال ولا يُبقي باقية ترددٍ.

والشّرحُ يُستَعْملُ حقيقةً في شقِّ اللحمِ ومجازاً في الكشفِ والبيانِ وعلى هذا يكون المعنى أنَّ الله تعالى يجعلُ في عقلِ من يُرادُ هدايتهُ قبُولاً واستعداداً وتوفيقاً للإسلام حتى يسكُنَ إليهِ ويرضى به ومن هُنا يشبهُ بالشرحِ الذي هو انفتاح يُظِهرُ ما تحتَهُ، فلا يبقى معه أثر شكٍ أو ترددٍ.

وقد روى الطبراني وغيره عن ابن مسعود رضي الله عنه أن ناسا قالوا: يا رسولَ الله، كيف يشرح الله صدره للإسلام؟ فقال رسول الله ﷺ: ''يُدْخِلُ فيه النور فينْفَسِح.'' قالوا: وهل لذلك من علامةٍ يُعرَفُ بها؟ قال: ''الإِنابَةُ إلى دارِ الخُلُودِ والتَّنحي عن دار الغرور والاستعدادُ للموتِ قبل

before death comes."[11] Naturally, the word "expands" in the hadith is not meant literally, for the breast does not actually grow larger; that is not possible. What it means is that the heart acquires acceptance and tranquility, and its desire for Islam strengthens because it perceives the beauty of it.

Other subtle lessons of this parable include:

(1) The servant of God is granted goodness in two ways: his soul inclines toward the good and desires it, and he is rewarded and benefited as a result of it. This is from the tremendous mercy of God, because if a person is obliged to do something without having any desire or motivation in his soul to do it, he may experience great suffering and distress.

In His great kindness, God Most High instills psychological motivation in His servant's soul, and he acts upon that motivation and thereby achieves goodness and reward. The reason He does this is to make it easier for the servant to engage in acts of worship and obedience, and to open to him the doors of virtue so that his ennoblement may be perfected. ʿUmar ibn ʿAbd al-ʿAzīz[12] ﷺ said, "When one's desire corresponds to the truth, it is like honey mixed with butter. Whoever moves toward God by his natural inclination, his reaching Him is closer to him than his own nature is."

(2) The parable illustrates how the human being is honored by having the beauty of the truth shown to him, so that his soul may be at peace. He is a creature of great value, having been granted intelligence by which he may recognize the truth, provided that it is divested of base desire and evil inclinations. If he does so, then he has been chosen to uphold the right of this supreme blessing for which God has singled him out.

11: Ḥākim, *Mustadrak* 7863.

12: ʿUmar ibn ʿAbd al-ʿAzīz (d. 101/720) was the eighth Umayyad caliph, famous for his justice and righteousness.

الفوت." قلت: ولاشكَّ أن معنى 'ينفَسِح' في الحديث ليس على الحقيقة، إذ لا يوسع الصدرُ حقيقة لأنه محالٌ وإنما معناه حصول القبول والراحة فيه وتقوية الرغبة فيه لما يرى من محاسنه.

ومِنْ لطائف هذا المثل إضافة لما سبق:

(١) الجمعُ للعبد في الأمر الخير بين مَيل النفسِ وحصول الرغبة مع ترتب الثواب والنفع على ذلك وهو من عظيم رحمة الله. ألا ترى أن المرء إذا توجب عليه فعلُ شيء دون أقبال نفسٍ وحصولِ باعثٍ حصلَ له من ذلك تكدرٌ عظيم وغُصةٌ شديدةٌ. فمن عظيم لطف الله تعالى أن ركّبَ في العبد الباعث النفسي فيتحركُ العبد بناءً عليه فيحصل له الخير والثواب. وإنما جعلَ ذلك لتسهلِ للعبدُ الأعمال والطاعات وتنفتح عليه أبواب الفضل فتَكْمُلَ كرامَتُهُ. قال عمر بن عبد العزيز (رضي الله عنه): إذا وافق الحق الهوى فذلك الشهد بالزبد؛ ومَن سارَ إلى الله بطَبعِه كان الوصول أقرَب إليه من طبعه.

(٢) تكريم الإنسان في إظهار جمال الحق له كي تطمئن نفسه إذ هو مخلوق ذو قيمةٍ مُنحَ عقلاً يعرفُ الحقَّ إذا خُلّيَ عن الهوى ونوازِع الشر، فيكون بهذا مُختارا قائما بحق هذه النعمةِ العُظمى التي مَيّزَهُ الله بها.

Parable 10: The Narrowness of Unbelief

Sūrat al-An'ām (6), Verse 125

And when He desires to lead someone astray, He makes his breast narrow and constricted, as though he were climbing skywards.

This parable depicts the state of the idolater and his aversion to Islam and his heart's exasperation by it whenever he is called to it or considers it when it is presented to him. It likens this to the state of a person who tries to climb up into the sky and is extremely put off by doing so, or someone who actually does climb up into the sky and feels his breast narrowing, as though his spirit will leave his body due to the effect of that ascent. Either way, he will experience difficulty and heaviness, which is the common element between the two scenarios.

The word *ḥaraj* (constricted) literally means a place so densely forested that it is impossible to reach. The meaning, then, is that He makes that person's breast closed off so that no goodness can enter it, nor can any light find a way into it. It is related that Ibn 'Abbās ﷺ recited this verse and then said, "Is there anyone from the Bakr tribe here?" A man replied, "I am." He asked him, "What does *ḥaraja* mean in your dialect?" He replied, "A valley with many tangled trees, in which there is no pathway." Ibn 'Abbās said, "Such is the heart of the unbeliever."

The word can also be read as *ḥarij*, which means "extremely narrow", indicating that God makes that person's breast as narrow

المثلُ العاشر: وضيقُ الكفر
سورة الأنعام الآية (١٢٥)

﴿ وَمَنْ يُرِدْ أَنْ يُضِلَّهُ يَجْعَلْ صَدْرَهُ ضَيِّقًا حَرَجًا كَأَنَّمَا يَصَّعَّدُ فِي السَّمَاءِ ﴾

في هذا المثل شبه حال المشرك في نفوره من الإسلام وضيقِ قلبه به حين يُدعى إليه أُوْ يَتَأملهُ حين يعرضُ عليه بحالِ شخصٍ كُلِّفَ الصعودَ في السماءِ فَعَظُمتْ نفرَته من ذلك أو يصعَدُ فيها فضاق صدره وكادت روحه تخرُجُ من آثارِ ذلك الصعود. ففي كلا الأمرين حصول مشقة وثقل وهو الجامع بين الصورتين.

والحَرَجُ -بفتحتين- مكانٌ كثُرَت أشجارُهُ حتى لم يعد يستطيع أن يصل إليه أحد فيكون المعنى يجعل صدره مغلقا لا يدخُلُهُ خير ولا يتسللِ إليه نور. روي عن ابن عباس (رضي الله عنهما) أنّهُ قرأ هذه الآية وقال: هل ههنا أحدٌ من بني بكر؟ قال رجلٌ: نعم. قال: ما الحَرَجَةُ فيكم؟ قال: الوادي الكثير الشجرِ المشتبك الذي لا طريق فيه. فقال ابن عباس: كذلك قلب الكافر.

وقُرِئَ: حَرِجاً - بكسر الراء- ومعناه شديد الضيق أي يجعل صدره ضيقا غاية في الضيق. وعلى كلا القراءتين،

as can be. Either way, what is meant is that the unbeliever's breast is narrow and averse to the truth, and no light can reach it.

Other subtleties of this parable include:

(1) The verse alludes to the shortness of breath that one experiences at high elevations, which was something known to the Arabs since their lands contained many mountains, and they had experienced this when climbing them. However, modern science has discovered the cause of this, which is that there is less oxygen at higher altitudes. The verse contains multiple levels of discourse, as befits each age.

(2) The word for "climbing" in this verse has several variant readings. Ibn Kathīr[13] reads *yaṣʿad*; Shuʿba reads it from ʿĀṣim[14] as *yaṣṣāʿad*, which is a variant pronunciation of *yataṣāʿad*. The majority read it as *yaṣṣaʿʿad*, which is a variant pronunciation of *yataṣaʿʿad*. All of these readings contain subtle nuances of meaning. Ibn Kathīr's reading simply denotes the act of climbing, without any further meaning; the reading of Shuʿba implies a sense of gradual climbing, little by little over a long period, suggesting that what is being climbed is high and difficult to surmount—the letter *alif* (long *ā*) in the verb form is what suggests this. The reading of the majority suggests the notion of climbing with difficulty and under duress, having to push oneself forward again and again. These different readings all depict the varying states of the unbelievers in their aversion, and how the weight of it differs between them, depending upon the strength of their antipathy to Islam and the extent to which unbelief has taken hold of their hearts.

13: Ibn Kathīr al-Makkī (d. 120/737) of Mecca was among the transmitters of the seven major canonical readings of the Qur'ān.

14: ʿĀṣim ibn Abīl-Najūd (d. 127/745) of Kufa was among the transmitters of the seven major canonical readings of the Qur'ān. Abū Bakr Shuʿba ibn ʿAyyāsh al-Nahshalī (d. 193/809) was one of the transmitters of the reading of ʿĀṣim.

فالمعنى أن صدر الكافر ضيق نافرٌ من الحق لا يصله من نوره شيء.

ومِنْ لطائفِ هذا المثل فضلا عما سبق ما يلي:

(١) أن الآية أشارت إلى ضيق تَنَفُّس مَنْ يصعدُ للعلو وهوَ أمرٌ كان معلوماً لدى العَرَبِ حيث توفرت الجبال في بلادهِم وعرفوا ذلك من صعودها بالتجربة، غير أن العلم الحديث كشف عن سرِّ ذلك حيث ينقص غاز الأكسجين فتعدَّدَ مستوى الخطاب في الآية بما يناسب كلَّ عصر.

(٢) أن كلمة 'يصعد' قُرِئت في الآية بعدد منِ القراءات، فقرأ ابنُ كثيرٍ 'يَصْعَدُ' ساكنةَ الصادِ وقرأ شعبةُ عن عاصم 'يَصَّاعَدُ' وأصلها يتصاعد وقرأ الجمهور 'يَصَّعَدُ' وأصلها يَتَصَعّدُ' وفي كلٍّ هذه القراءات معانٍ لطيفة. فقراءة ابن كثير تشير إلى نفس فعل الصعود دون زيادةٍ بينما تشير قراءة شعبة إلى الصعود شيئا فشيئا مع طول المدة وارتفاع ما يصعد إليه - يستفاد ذلك من الألف- وهو أثقل على فاعله أما قراءة الجمهور ففيها معنى الصعود مع المشقة والضيق مع دفع النفس دفعا. فظهر من تلك القراءات المختلفةِ تَعَدُّدُ أحوالِ الكفار في نفرتهم واختلاف ثقله عليهم بحسب كراهيتهم له وتمكنِ الكفرِ من قلوبهم.

Parable 11: Good Land and Bad Land

Sūrat al-Aʿrāf (7), Verse 58

As for the good land, its vegetation comes forth by permission of its Lord; and as for the bad, it comes forth only miserably.

This verse contains a parable depicting the differing states of people in how they benefit from God's guidance and mercy, comparing them to two different kinds of land. One kind is good and has healthy soil, and so it benefits from rain and quickly gives forth splendid crops. The other is bad and barren and can barely produce anything; the most it might yield is a small quantity of bad crops which provide no benefit.

In this parable, God likens the believer and unbeliever to fertile land and salty land, and the revelation of the Qur'ān to the sending down of rain. He compares the believer to fertile land which benefits from the rain that falls upon it and gives forth all manner of flowers and fruits. The unbeliever, in contrast, is like salty land which produces only a little. The believer's spirit is pure and untainted by poor character traits, and so when the light of Revelation connects with it, all manner of righteous action and knowledge arises in it. But when the light connects with the foul polluted spirit, nothing is reflected back.

The word *nakid* (miserably) literally means a miser who stingily

المثلُ الحادي عشر: البلد الطيب والبلد الخبيث
سورةُ الأعراف الآية (٥٨)

﴿ وَالْبَلَدُ الطَّيِّبُ يَخْرُجُ نَبَاتُهُ بِإِذْنِ رَبِّهِ وَالَّذِي خَبُثَ لَا يَخْرُجُ إِلَّا نَكِدًا ﴾

تشتملُ هذه الآيةُ على تمثيلٍ لاختلافِ حال الناس في الانتفاعِ بهدى الله ورحمته ببلدين مختلفين أحدُهما طيب صالحُ التربةِ ينتفعُ بالغيثِ فينبتُ سريعا بَهِجاً والآخرُ خبيث عقيمٌ لا يَكادُ يُنبِتُ وإنْ أنْبتَ أخرَجَ نَبْتا قلِيلاً خبيثاً لا نفعَ فيه.

فُهُوَ مثلٌ ضرَبَهُ الله للمؤمن والكافرِ بالأَرضِ الخيِّرَة والأرض السبخةِ فشبّه نزولَ القرآن بنُزُولِ المطرِ وشبه المؤمنَ بالأرض الخيرة التي ينزلُ عليها المطر فتنتفعُ به وتحصل فيها أنواعُ الأزهار والثمار أما الكافر فهو مثل الأرض السبخة التي لا يحصل فيها من النبات إلا القليل. فروحُ المُؤمنِ طاهرةٌ نقيةٌ عن الأخلاق الذميمةِ إذا اتصلَ بها نورُ الوحي ظهرت فيها أنواع الطاعات والمعارف أما الرّوحُ الكَدِرَةُ الخبيثةُ فهي وإن اتصل بها النورُ لم تعكس شيئا.

والنَّكِدُ في اللغةِ العَسِرُ المُمْتَنِعُ من إعطاءِ الخيرِ على جِهَةِ البُخْلِ وقال الليثُ: الشُؤْمُ واللؤْمُ وقلَّةُ العطاءِ. وقد قرأ

refuses to give anything good. Layth[15] says that it means 'inauspicious, mean, and miserly.' The Medinans recited the word here as *nakad*, the rest *nakid*. Zajjāj[16] says that there are two other forms of the word, *nakd* and *nukd*, although they do not feature in any canonical recitations.

Other subtleties of this verse include:

(1) It summarizes what is described in detail in an authentic Prophetic hadith narrated by Imam al-Bukhārī, who related on the authority of Abū Mūsā al-Ash'arī ﵁ that the Prophet ﷺ said, "The guidance and knowledge with which God has sent me are like rain that falls upon land. The fertile portion of the land absorbs the water and brings forth much grass and herbs. The arid land retains the water, and God benefits people with it so that they may drink, water their animals, and irrigate. The rest falls into an abyss, which neither retains the water nor produces plants. Such (the former) is the likeness of someone who understands God's religion and benefits from that with which God has sent me, learning and teaching others. Then there is the one who neither raises his head to [listen to] it nor accepts God's guidance with which I have been sent."[17]

(2) This verse contains the rhetorical feature known as *iḥtibāk* (interlacing), which is when two contrasting things are mentioned with an element removed from each one which is reflected in what is retained of the other. For example, a poet said, 'I fed them straw and cool water', meaning 'and I watered them with cool water.' The way it is employed in this verse is that He does not describe the vegetation of the good land as good, and He does not mention the bad land before the bad vegetation, since each of them is implied by the mention of its opposite. So what is implied in full is, 'The vegetation

15: Layth ibn Naṣr or ibn al-Muẓaffar (d. after 170/786) was a grammarian of Basra.
16: Abū Isḥāq al-Zajjāj (d. 310/922) was a grammarian and theologian of Basra.
17: Bukhārī, *Ṣaḥīḥ* 79; Muslim, *Ṣaḥīḥ* 2282.

أهلُ المدينةِ نَكَداً بفتح الكاف وقرأَ العامةُ بِكَسْرِهَا. قالَ الزجاجُ: وفيهِ وجْهَانِ آخَرَانِ لَمْ يُقْرَأْ بِهِما: 'نَكْداً' و 'نُكْداً'.

وفي الآيةِ معانٍ لطيفة زيادة على ما سبق:

(١) أنّها جمعت ما فصّلَهُ الحديثُ النبويُ الصحيح الذي أخرجه الإمام البخاري من رواية أبي موسى الأشعري (رضي الله عنه) عن النبي ﷺ قال: "مَثَلُ مَا بَعَثَنِي اللَّهُ بِهِ مِنَ الْهُدَى وَالعِلْمِ كَمَثَلِ الْغَيْثِ الْكَثِيرِ أَصَابَ أَرْضًا، فَكَانَ مِنْهَا نَقِيَّةٌ قَبِلَتِ الْمَاءَ، فَأَنْبَتَتِ الْكَلأَ وَالْعُشْبَ الْكَثِيرَ، وَكَانَتْ مِنْهَا أَجَادِبُ أَمْسَكَتِ الْمَاءَ، فَنَفَعَ اللَّهُ بِهَا النَّاسَ، فَشَرِبُوا وَسَقَوْا وَزَرَعُوا، وَأَصَابَتْ مِنْهَا طَائِفَةً أُخْرَى، إِنَّمَا هِيَ قِيعَانٌ لاَ تُمْسِكُ مَاءً، وَلاَ تُنْبِتُ كَلأً، فَذَلِكَ مَثَلُ مَنْ فَقِهَ فِي دِينِ اللَّهِ وَنَفَعَهُ مَا بَعَثَنِي اللَّهُ بِهِ، فَعَلِمَ وَعَلَّمَ، وَمَثَلُ مَنْ لَمْ يَرْفَعْ بِذَلِكَ رَأْسًا، وَلَمْ يَقْبَلْ هُدَى اللَّهِ الَّذِي أُرْسِلْتُ بِهِ."

(٢) في الآية احتباكٌ والاحتباكُ هو أن يجتمع في الكلام متقابلان ويُحذَف من كلِّ واحدٍ منهما مقابله لدلالة الآخر عليه مثل قول الشاعر: علفتها تبناً وماءاً بارِداً (أي وسقيتها ماءاً). وتفصيله في الآية أنه لم يذكر وصف الطيب بعد نبات البلد الطيب ولم يذكُر الأرض الخبيثة قبل ذكر النبات الخبيث لدلالة كلا الضدين على الآخر. والتقدير: والبلدُ الطيب يخرجُ نباته طيباً بإذنِ ربّه والنباتُ الذي خَبُثَ يَخرُجُ نكداً من البلدِ الخبيثِ. قلتُ: والاحتباكُ فنٌّ بلاغيٌ دقيقٌ من فنونِ البديع يجري في كلام العرب وليس هذا محلَّ بسط الحديث فيه فراجعهُ إن شئتَ في كتبِ البلاغة.

of the good land comes forth good, and the vegetation which is bad comes forth miserably from the bad land.' I would add that *iḥtibāk* is one of the subtle rhetorical devices of the Arabic language, but this is not the place for a comprehensive study of it. One may consult the works on Arabic rhetoric for more.

(3) The verse highlights the importance of preparing one's heart and one's outward being to receive God's guidance, so that its fruits may be reaped. It also points to the importance of selecting people of talent and aptitude for teachers, spouses, and other functions. That is because the message has one source and is watered with one water, but benefiting from it and absorbing its teachings and directions depends upon the state of the heart and the soul. Our Glorious Lord says, *They are watered by the same water, but We make some of them excel others in flavor* [Qur'ān 13:4].

(٣) في الآية تنبيهٌ على أهمية استعداد القلوب والقوالب لاستقبال هدى الله كي يحصلُ ثمرها وهي إشارة لأهمية اختيار أصحاب الملكات والاستعداد في التعليم والزواج وغيرها. وذلك لأن الرسالة معدنها واحد وماؤها واحد لكن الانتفاع بها وتعاطي أحكامها وتوجيهاتها يكون بحسب حال القلب والنفس. قال ربنا جلَّ وعلا: ''**يُسْقَى بِمَاءٍ وَاحِدٍ وَنُفَضِّلُ بَعْضَهَا عَلَى بَعْضٍ فِي الْأُكُلِ.**'' (الرعد: ٤)

Parable 12: The Panting Dog

Sūrat al-Aʿrāf (7), Verses 175-176

Tell them the tale of the one to whom We gave Our Signs, but he shook them off, so Satan overtook him and he became one of the lost. Had We willed, We would have elevated him thereby, but he clung to the earth and followed his caprices. His likeness is that of a dog; if you shoo it, it pants, and if you leave it be, it pants.

This verse contains a compound parable, depicting the state of someone who strove and sought the truth until he was guided to it, and cast off idolatry early on before the Message was revealed and he was called to submit to it; but then he became exposed to the whisperings of Satan, who tempted him back to idolatry, and so he rejected the call of truth when he was summoned by it and it reached him, and he abandoned the goodness which he had attained, and pursued his base desire. The parable compares him to a dog which is always panting whether it is shooed away and beaten or left alone. In either case he is wretched, for having taken on something which he was not bidden to do, but then refused when it was required of him to do it.

The elements of this parable are as follows: the errant person is compared to a panting dog; his wretchedness and confusion during his time of searching for religion is compared to the panting of a dog when it is let be; and his wretchedness when rejecting the true religion when it finally arrives is compared to the panting of a dog

المثلُ الثاني عشر: كـ: الكلب اللاهث
سورةُ الأعراف الآية (١٧٥-١٧٦)

﴿ وَاتْلُ عَلَيْهِمْ نبَأَ الَّذِي آتيْنَاهُ آيَاتِنَا فَانْسَلَخَ مِنْهَا فَأَتْبَعَهُ الشَّيْطَانُ فَكَانَ مِنَ الْغَاوِينَ وَلَوْ شِئْنَا لَرَفَعْنَاهُ بِهَا وَلَكِنَّهُ أَخْلَدَ إِلَى الْأَرْضِ وَاتَّبَعَ هَوَاهُ فَمَثَلُهُ كَمَثَلِ الْكَلْبِ إِنْ تَحْمِلْ عَلَيْهِ يَلْهَثْ أَوْ تَتْرُكْهُ يَلْهَثْ ﴾

تشتملُ هذه الآية على تشبيه مركب مثّل فيه حال من تعَنّى وبحث عن الحق حتى اهتدى إليه ونبذَ الشرك في مبدأ أمره قبل ظهور أمر الرسالة ومطالبته بها ثم تَعرّض لوساوس الشيطان فحسّن له الشرك فرفض دعوة الحق حين طولب بها وبلغته فانسلخ من ذلك الخير الذي كان عليه واتبع هواه، بحال الكلب اللاهث على الدوام سواء حُمل عليه فطرد أو ضرب أو ترك في دعةٍ. فهو شقيٌّ في الحالين بتكلُّف ما لم يُطالبْ بها ثم برفض ذلك حين طولب به.

وأجزاء هذا التشبيه هي أن يشبه ذلك الضال بالكلب اللاهث، ويشبه شقاؤه واضطراب أمره في مدة بحثه عن الدين بلهث الكلب حال تركه في دعةٍ ويشبه شقاؤُه في إعراضهِ عن الدّين الحق عند مجيئه بلهث الكلب في حالِ طردِه وضربه.

ولهذا التشبيه قصة وسبب تكلم فيها علماء

when it is shooed off and beaten.

There is a true story behind this parable, which has been discussed by the commentators. The soundest version,[18] as far as I can tell, is that it refers to one of two men, or else to both of them. The first was Umayya ibn Abīl-Ṣalt al-Thaqafī, who was an Arab poet and a leading figure of the tribe of Thaqīf. In the age of pagan ignorance he searched for the true religion, examining the Torah and Gospels before becoming a *ḥanīf* [an adherent of Abrahamic monotheism] and an ascetic, forbidding himself wine. He composed much poetry and traveled extensively, and he predicted that a Prophet would soon come, while hoping that it would be him. When Umayya heard that the Messenger of God ﷺ had emerged, he went to him and listened to him, but refused to believe in him out of envy and a desire to conceal the truth. He went as far as to eulogize the idolaters who were slain at the Battle of Badr. He then returned to Ṭā'if and died there as an unbeliever.

The second was Abū ʿĀmir al-Nuʿmān ibn Ṣayfī al-Khazrajī [of Medina], a monk who converted to Christianity before the coming of the Messenger of God ﷺ and claimed to be a follower of the *ḥanīf* way. When God's Messenger ﷺ came to Medina, he asked him, 'Muḥammad, what is it that you have brought?' He replied, 'I have brought the *ḥanīf* way, the religion of Abraham.' He said, 'I already follow it.' The Prophet ﷺ said, 'You do not, for you have introduced foreign elements to it.' Abū ʿĀmir rejected this and out of envy and bitterness refused to follow the Prophet ﷺ, his base desire preventing him from accepting the truth, though before the coming of the Message he had sought it. He made for Mecca to encourage the people there to fight our master the Messenger of God ﷺ.

18: Author's note: My preference for this version is not based on my own opinion; rather, I follow the preference of ʿAllāma Muḥammad al-Ṭāhir Ibn ʿĀshūr (d. 1973) in his Qur'ān commentary *al-Taḥrīr wal-tanwīr*, where he prefers the opinion that the person meant in the verse was a man of renown among the Arabs. The first opinion was related from ʿAbd Allāh ibn ʿAmr and Zayd ibn Aslam. Al-Qurṭubī said that it is the most prevalent and well-known opinion. The second opinion was related from Saʿīd ibn al-Musayyab.

التفسير أَرْجَحُها[٢] - فيما تبين لي- أنه يشير إلى واحد من اثنين أو كليهما:

الأول: أميةُ بن أبي الصَّلْت الثقفي. كان شاعرا من شعراء العرب ومقدما في قبيلة ثقيف وكان قد بحث عن دين الحقِ في الجاهليةِ ونظرَ في التوراة والإنجيل ثمَّ تحَنَّفَ وتزَهَّدَ وحرَّم الخمر وقال شعرا كثيرا وسافر وكان يُخبِرُ أنَّ نبيا قد أظلَّ زمانهُ ويؤَمَّلُ أن يكون ذلك النبي. فلما بلغهُ خروجِ رسول الله ﷺ أتاه وسمع منه ثم لم يؤمن به حسداً وكُفراً بل ورثى قتلى المشركين في بدرٍ ورجعَ إلى الطائف ومات على كفره.

والثاني: أبي عامر النعمان بن صيفي الخزرجي الراهب تنصر قبل مبعث رسول الله ﷺ وزعم أنه على الحنيفية فلما قدم رسول الله ﷺ المدينة قال: يا محمد ما الذي جئت به؟ قال: جئتُ بالحنيفيةِ دينِ إبراهيم. قال: فإني عليها. فقال النبي ﷺ له: لست عليها لأنك أدخَلتَ فيها ما ليس منها. فَكَفَرَ ورفضَ أن يُتابِعَ النبي ﷺ حسدا وغِلّا وصده هواه عن الحق بعد أن طلبه قبل البعثة وخرج إلى مكة يُحرِّض على قتال سيدنا رسول الله ﷺ وانهزم ثم خرج للشام وهلك بها.

وفي الآية زيادة على ما قلناه جملة من الفوائد:

(١) أن الله تعالى شبه ذلك الضال بالكلب اللاهث فالتشبيه ليس بالكلب فقط، بل بالكلب الذي يلهث في الحالين حال

٢: ترجيحي لهذا ليس استقلالا وإنما هو اتباع لاختيار العلامة محمد الطاهر بن عاشور في تفسيره التحرير والتنوير حيث رجح أن المعنيَّ بالآية رجلٌ ممن للعرب إلمامٌ بهم. ورُويَ القولُ الأولُ عن عبد الله بن عمرو وزيد بن أسلم وقال القرطبي هو الأشهر وقول الأكثر. وأما القول الثاني فقد رويَ عن سعيد بن المسيب.

After suffering defeat, he went to Syria, where he died.

Other lessons of this verse include:

(1) God Most High likens that errant man to a panting dog—not just any dog, but specifically a dog which pants whether it is left alone or shooed away. The point of comparison is that the errant man took it upon himself to follow the true religion while he was in a situation in which this had not been demanded of him, and he endured hardship and strife in pursuit of it.

But then when the time to follow that truth arrived, with the appearance of the Final Prophet ﷺ, he brought misery upon himself by stubbornly opposing him and rejecting him, instead of gaining the satisfaction of attaining his goal. In this he resembled a dog which pants at the time when panting is appropriate, namely when it is shooed and threatened, but also goes on panting when that is not the case and it is left in peace.

(2) This parable is one of the Holy Qur'ān's ingenious passages, because it also expresses the inner turmoil of that errant man and the constriction of his soul, just as the dog's inner turmoil and shortness of breath makes it pant all the time. The dog is an intelligent animal in which there is a certain combination of servility, loyalty, and cowardice. It follows its owner whether he starves it or feeds it, and it guards him and keeps watch, alerting him with its barking. It sleeps little by night and much by day, and calms itself by panting due to its shortness of breath.

The Arabs would sometimes name their sons Kalb (dog) as a good omen. A father might go out for a walk after his son was born, and if he saw a dog he would name the child Kalb, or choose a different name depending upon what he saw. The reason why the dog was seen as a good omen was that it was hoped that the child would grow up to be vigilant, guarding and protecting his family.

الدعة وحال الطرد. ووجه التمثيل أن هذا الضال تحمل اتباع الدين الصالح وهو في حالٍ لم يكلف فيها بذلك وصار يطلبهُ في عناءٍ ونصب؛ فلما حان اتباع ذلك الحق بخروج النبي الخاتم ﷺ حمل نفسه الشقاء بعناده واعراضه بدلا من أن يستريح لحصول مطلوبه فأشبه حال الكلب الموصوف باللهث حال وجود ما يستدعي اللهث من طرد وتخويف وبقاء ذلك اللهث أيضا حال الخلو من ذلك وتركه في مسالمة.

(٢) هذا التشبيه من مُبتكرات القرآن الكريم وذلك لأنه عبَّر فيه أيضا عن اضطراب باطن هذا الضال وضيقِ نَفْسِهِ كما أن اضطراب باطن الكلب وضيق مجاريه يجعله في حال لُهاثٍ دائمٍ. والكلبُ حيوانٌ ذكيٌّ فيه لؤمٌ ونَذالةٌ مَعَ وفاءٍ وجُبنٍ يَتْـبَـعُ من يُجيعُهُ ومن يُطْعِمُهُ يحرسُ ويحفظُ ويُنَبِّهُ بنُباحه، قليل نوم الليل كثير نوم النهار يرتاح باللهث لضيق مجاري نفسه. وقد سمى العرب بعض أولادهم كلباً من باب التفاؤل حيث كان الواحدُ منهم إذا ولدَ له خرج وسار فإن رأى كلبا سمى ولده كلبا، أو رأي غير ذلك سماه بحسب ما رأى. وسببُ تفاؤلِهِم بالكلبِ أَنْ يكونَ الولُد يَقِظاً يحرسُ أهله ويرعاهم.

Parable 13: The Weight of Pleasures

Sūrat al-Tawba (9), Verse 38

O you who believe, what is wrong with you that when you are told to go forth in God's cause, you sink down heavily to the earth?

This verse depicts the state of those who were reluctant to go out to fight and who looked for excuses so that they could stay behind instead of joining the Messenger of God ﷺ in jihad. It compares them to someone who is asked to get up but responds by clinging to the ground and staying fast there, refusing even to get up, much less to go out.

Heaviness is a state in a body which causes it to strongly seek to move downwards, and makes it difficult to transport. Here it is used figuratively to denote sluggishness.

This verse was revealed in connection with the Expedition of Tabūk, when the Messenger of God ﷺ set out with the Muslims in extremely hot weather and embarked upon a long journey with the intention of fighting the Byzantines, having made his intention plain to them so that they would prepare, though usually it was his ﷺ custom to conceal his intentions when going to battle.

When the time came to set out, some of the Muslims were reluctant, some hesitant, and some refused to go altogether, happy to remain in pleasant shade amid ample fruits, despite the Prophet's ﷺ dire need for support and numbers. When he ﷺ returned, some of them offered their excuses, whether sincere or insincere. Three

المثلُ الثالثُ عشر: أثقال الملذات
سورةُ التوبةِ الآية (٣٨)

﴿ يَا أَيُّهَا الَّذِينَ آمَنُوا مَا لَكُمْ إِذَا قِيلَ لَكُمُ انْفِرُوا فِي سَبِيلِ اللَّهِ اثَّاقَلْتُمْ إِلَى الْأَرْضِ ﴾

هذه الآيةُ تمثيلٌ لحالِ الكارهينَ للغَزوِ الباحثينَ عَنْ عُذرٍ ليَقْعُدوا عن الخروجِ للجهادِ معَ رسول الله ﷺ بحالِ مَنْ يُطلَبُ منه النهوضُ فيقابلُ ذلكَ بالالتصاقِ في الأرضِ والتمكنِ من القعودِ، فيأبى النهوضَ فضلاً عن السيرِ. والثقلُ حالةُ في الجسم تقتضي شدة تطلبه النزول إلى أسفل وعسر انتقاله وهو مستعمل هنا في البطء مجازاً.

وقد نَزَلَتْ هذه الآية في غزوة تبوك حيث استنفرَ رسولِ الله ﷺ المسلمين في وقت شديد الحر واستقبل سفراً بعيداً حيث كان خارجا لقتال الروم وقد جلّى لهم وجهته ليتأهبوا. وكان من عادته صلوات الله وسلامه عليه إن أراد الخروجَ أن يُورّيَ عن وجهته فلما كان وقتُ الخروجِ تثاقلَ بَعْضُهم وتقاعَسَ بعضهم وتخلف البعض بالكليةِ رضا بالظلّ الظليل والثمار الوافرة مع شدةِ حاجته صلوات الله وسلامه عليه إلى النصر والظهرِ والعُدّةِ. ولمَّا عادَ صلوات الله عليه

Companions who had stayed behind for no good reason came and confessed this, and the Prophet ﷺ ordered that they be estranged until their repentance had become sincere and God had relented to them and confirmed this with a revelation of the Qur'ān.

The subtleties of this verse include:

(1) It alludes to man's origin and how he was created from clay, though the secret of his humanity lies in his resistance of that terrestrial attachment, which is achieved by reducing one's engagement in those things which distract and obstruct one from the means of spiritual growth and acceptance.

(2) God's Words *to the earth* allude to how everything which distracts us from heeding the calls of truth is located in and confined to the earth. What kind of soul would be content to sacrifice that which is loftier for that which is earthbound?

The choice of the word 'earth' is ingenious for another reason, which is that it alludes to the motive for their hesitancy on that occasion, which was that they desired to remain in their orchards amid their fruits, which are things of the earth.

(3) Consider also how He uses the verb *iththāqala*, which is a variant of *tathāqala* in the *tafāʿala* perfect tense form [Form VI], with the initial letter *tā'* transformed into a *thā'* because of the proximity of their places of articulation and certain common qualities of their pronunciation such as *hams* (whispering) and *istifāl* (lowering the tongue from the palate).

The two *thā'*s are then combined in one geminated letter [as *tathāqala* instead of *taththāqala*], and a *hamzat al-waṣl* is added at the start to allow pronunciation from a pause. The gemination and the addition of the *hamza* add physicality to the sense of heaviness inherent in the verb, and the notion of attachment to something superfluous and ephemeral such as worldly wealth. The form of the verb itself alludes to the manifold types of heaviness: heaviness of

اعتَذَرَ من اعتَذَرَ كاذِباً أو صادِقاً وجاء ثلاثةُ من الصحابة تَخَلَّفوا بلا عُذْرٍ فاعتَرَفوا بأنهُ لا عُذْرَ لهم فأمرَ رسولِ الله ﷺ بمُقَاطَعَتِهِمْ حتَّى صَحَّتْ تَوْبَتُهُم وتابَ اللهُ عليهم وأَنْزَلَ في ذلِكَ قُرآناً يُتْلى.

وَمِن لطائِفِ هذه الآية:

(١) الإشارة إلى أصلِ الإِنسانِ وأنّهُ مخلوقٌ من طِينٍ إلا أنَّ السرَّ في إنسانيتهِ يكْمُنُ في مكافَحَتِهِ هذا التَّعَلُّقَ الطينيِّ وذلك بالتخفف عما يُشغِلهُ ويُعَطِّله عن دواعي الإنابه وأسباب الاستجابةِ.

(٢) أن في قوله تعالى: (إلى الأَرْضِ) إشارةً إلى أن كُلَّ ما يُشغِل عن الاستماع لداعي الحق محلهُ ومُنتهاه للأرض فأيُّ نفسٍ ترضى أَنْ تُضحي بالعليا من أجل شيءٍ محله الأرضِ. ثم إنَّ اختيارَ لفظِ الأَرضِ بديعٌ من حيثُ كونِهِ مشيراً لباعِثِ التباطؤِ في تلكَ الحالةِ وهو الرغبةُ في البقَاءِ في حَوَائِطِهِم وثِمَارِهِم وهذهِ من الأَرضِ.

(٣) ثُمَّ انظُر- يا رعاكَ الله- إلى اختيارِ هذا الفعل (اثَّاقَلَ) وأصله تَثَاقَل على وزن (تَفَاعَلَ) فعلٌ ماضٍ قُلِبَتْ تاؤُهُ ثاءً لقُربِ المَخرَجِ والاشتراك في بعضِ الصفاتِ كالهَمسِ والاستفالِ ثم أُدْغِمَتْ في الثاءِ الأُخرَى ثمَّ زيدَت همزَةُ الوَصلِ في أَوّلِهِ كيْ يُتَوَصَّلَ بها للنُّطقِ بالساكِنِ.

ودلَالةُ الإدغام وزيادة الهمزة كفيلتان ببيانِ جسامةِ هذا الفعل والتعلق بالزائدِ الزائل من المتاع. بل إن في صيغة

wealth, heaviness of attachment to family and home, heaviness of the fear of death, in addition to the heaviness of the fleshly body itself and its desire and avarice. How ingenious this verb is, and how profound are its meanings!

الفعل إشارة لتعدد أنواع الثقل؛ ثقل المال، وثقل التعلق بالذرية والديار، وثقل الخوف من الموت، فضلا عن ثقل الجسم واللحم والدعة والرغبة والطمع. فما أبدع هذا الفعل وأعمقَ معانيه.

Parable 14: The Reality of Life in This World
Sūrat Yūnus (10), Verse 24

The likeness of life in this world is none other than that of water which We send down from the sky, so that it mingles with the plants of the earth from which men and cattle eat, until, when the earth takes on its luster and is adorned, and its folk think that they are masters of it, Our command comes upon it by night or day, and We reduce it to stubble, as if it had not flourished the day before. Thus do We detail the signs for people who reflect.

This verse compares the state of the present life and the swiftness of its passing, how its finery fades after having been splendid and fresh, to the state of the plants of the earth and how they are watered and grown only to become chaff, reduced to stubble. This is a very beautiful and impactful parable which vividly illustrates the insignificance and paltriness of the present life and how swiftly it degenerates. To someone who enjoys the present world and relies upon it, it is like a fresh plant which grows strong after its quickening and gives forth manifold fruits, but is then taken away from him, leaving him in great anguish. The verse depicts this in great detail, to the benefit of the listener and the pleasure of the attentive reader.

The subtleties of this parable include:

(1) The verse prefixes the parable with the phrase *innamā* (nothing other than), which in Arabic is called *al-qaṣr* (restriction), the

المثلُ الرابعِ عَشَر: حقيقة الحياة الدنيا
سورةُ يونس الآية (٢٤)

﴿ إِنَّمَا مَثَلُ الْحَيَاةِ الدُّنْيَا كَمَاءٍ أَنزَلْنَاهُ مِنَ السَّمَاءِ فَاخْتَلَطَ بِهِ نَبَاتُ الْأَرْضِ مِمَّا يَأْكُلُ النَّاسُ وَالْأَنْعَامُ حَتَّى إِذَا أَخَذَتِ الْأَرْضُ زُخْرُفَهَا وَازَّيَّنَتْ وَظَنَّ أَهْلُهَا أَنَّهُمْ قَادِرُونَ عَلَيْهَا أَتَاهَا أَمْرُنَا لَيْلًا أَوْ نَهَارًا فَجَعَلْنَاهَا حَصِيدًا كَأَنْ لَمْ تَغْنَ بِالْأَمْسِ كَذَلِكَ نُفَصِّلُ الْآيَاتِ لِقَوْمٍ يَتَفَكَّرُونَ ﴾

في هذه الآية شُبِّهَت حالةُ الحياة الدنيا في سرعةِ تقَضِّيها وزوالِ نعيمها بعد البهجة بها وتزايدِ نضارَتها بحالِ نباتِ الأرضِ في سقياه ونُمُوِّهِ ثم ذهابِهِ حُطاماً ومصيرِهِ حصيداً. وهو تشبيهٌ بديعٌ جداً عظيمُ الأثر شديد الوقْعِ في التهوين من شأنِ الدُّنيا وبيان حقارَتِها وسرعةِ تولِّيها فكأنها للمتمتع بها المعوِّلِ عليها مثلَ زرعٍ نضير يشتدُّ عوده بعد أن تَبرقَ رُعُوده، وتتنوع ثمراته ثم يزول عن صاحبه فتعظُمَ حسراته وقد أطنبت الآية في بيان ذلك إطنابا يفيد السامع ويُمتعُ المتابع.

والتشبيهُ هنا فيه لطائف نُجْمِلُها فيما يلي:

purpose of which is to emphasize the point. This kind of *qaṣr* is called *qaṣr al-qalb* (restriction by inversion), which is based on the notion of presenting the interlocutor with something that is the opposite of what he believes, in order to correct him and redirect him towards the truth.

(2) This is a compound parable, its parts representing the stages of life. [i] The water falling from the sky represents the initial stage of life, infancy, which is a time of innocence and hope for life's comforts. [ii] The mingling of the water with the plants of the earth represents the budding of life in that it resembles the emergence of crops shortly after rainfall, when the lightning-flashes of hopes appear. This clause begins with the particle *fa-* (so), meaning "immediately after", which alludes to how quickly the plants begin to appear. [iii] the fact that those plants are eaten by humans and cattle symbolizes the human desire for consuming life's pleasures and enjoying its good things. The different levels of their aspirations in that regard are like the diverse types of plants. Some plants provide food for humans, symbolizing the higher concerns such as knowledge, leadership, renown, and fame. Others provide food for animals, symbolizing the lower appetites such as eating, drinking, sex, and so on, which are common to humans and animals alike. [iv] The earth taking on its luster and adornment represents the full development and maturity of benefit and how humans become engrossed in it, likening this to a woman who has adorned herself beautifully. [v] Death and the sudden seizing of the soul is then symbolized by how the plants are reduced to stubble when they have been reaped. This alludes to the end of life, and the fact that the only truly valuable things that a person can gain in his worldly life are those which will benefit him on the Day of Resurrection.

(3) The verse contains a metaphor, likening the earth to a woman when she wishes to adorn herself and so chooses her most elegant clothing and jewelry. The Arabs describe this using the verb "take

(١) أنَّ الآية قدمت التشبيه بصيغة عربية تسمى صيغةَ (القصرَ) والغرض من ذلك تأكيد المقصود ويسمى هذا النوع من القصر (قصر القلب) وهو ينبني على تنزيل المُخاطب منزلةَ من يعتَقِدُ عكسَ تلك الحالة فيكون المعنى تصحيح ما لديه وتوقيفه على وجه الحقِّ.

(٢) أنَّ هذا التشبيه مُرَكّب وتُمثلُ أجزاءه أطوارَ الحياة: [١] فالماءُ النازل من السماء يشبه ابتداء أطوار الحياة من وقت الصبا في الصفا والأمل في نعيم العيش [٢] واختلاطه بنبات الأرض يشبه إقبال زهرة الحياة لأنها مثل خروج الزرع بُعيدَ المطر حيث تلمعُ بروق الآمال وقد ابتدأت هذه الجملة بفاء التعقيب إيذانا بسرعة ظهور النّباتِ. [٣] وكونُ ذلك النبات مما يأكلُ الناس والأنعام فيه تشبيه لرغبات الناس في تناول لذائذ الحياة والتنعم بأطايبها و اختلاف مراتب هممهم في ذلك بأنواع النبات فمنه ما يقتاته الناس، إشارة إلى معالى الأمور كالعلم والرياسة والوجاهة والشهرة ومنه ما يقتاته الأنعام وهي الشهوات الدنية كالأكل والشرب والجماع وغيرها مما يشارك الإنسانَ فيه الحيوان. [٤] وأخذُ الأرضِ زخرفها فيه تشبيه بلوغ الانتفاع إلى أقصاه ونضوجه وانهماك الناس في ذلك بامرأة قد تزينت غاية الزينة [٥] ثم يشبه الموت أو الأخذ على غفلة بجعل النبات حصيداً أي محصودا. وفيه إشارة إلى خاتمة العمر وأن المعول على ما جناه الإنسان في دنياه مما ينفعه يوم القيامة.

(٣) وفي الآية استعارة مكنية حيث شبه الأرض بالمرأة حين

on."[19] The verse certainly features a very high degree of vividness and rhetorical brilliance.

(4) Addendum: to further elaborate upon this theme, let us quote some verses on the subject of the world's ephemerality and short-lived duration. Imam ʿAlī, may God ennoble his countenance, said:

The world is just a passing thing;
        The world has no power to endure;
The world is simply like a web
        That's been woven by a spider.
The only thing you need from it,
        O seeker, is your nourishment.
For by my life I swear that soon
        All those who are in it will die.

Abū Isḥāq Ismāʿīl ibn al-Qāsim, who went by the name of Abūl-ʿAtāhiyya,[20] said:

The house where dwell is one where
        No resident can long remain.
So many people have lodged here –
        then nights and days bore them away.
That's how we find the world to be,
        Bearing off people, emptying homes.
The world is a message for folk,
        No more than a loan in their hands;
So know this, and be sure of it:
        Someday the loan must be returned.

19: Similar to how English speakers say "makeup" or "makeover."
20: Abū Isḥāq Ismāʿīl ibn al-Qāsim, better known as Abūl-ʿAtāhiyya (d. 213/828), was an Abbasid-era Arab poet of Iraq.

تريد التزين فتحضر أفخر ثيابها من حلي وألوان. والعربُ يسمون هذا الفعل (أخذا) ولاشك أن الآية تحتوي من قوة التصوير وبديع المعاني ما يجلُّ عن الحصر.

(٤) تذييلٌ: ومما يَحسُنُ في هذا المقامِ أن نَذكُرَ بعضَ الأشعارِ في زوال الدنيا وقصر مدتها: يقول الإمام على كرم الله وجهه:

إنما الدنيا فناء
ليس للدنـيا ثبـوت
إنما الدنيا كبيت
نسجته العنكبوت
ولقد يكفيك منها
أيها الطالب قوت
ولعمري عن قليل
كل من فيها يموت

ويقول أبو إسحاق إسماعيل بن القاسم المعروف بأبي العتاهية رحمه الله:

إن دارا نـحـن فيها لـدارُ
ليس فيـها لمقـيم قـرارُ
كم وكم قد حلها من أناسٍ
ذهب الليل بهم والنهارُ
وكـذا الدنيـا على ما رأينا

Imam Quṭb al-Irshād ʿAbd Allāh ibn ʿAlawī al-Ḥaddād[21] ﷺ said:

How can one count on an abode that is really
Like a phantom in a dream or the shade of a cloud?
Its appearance is false, its presence deceptive;
Its ending is death, which ties up all the world.
All that it gathers fades; all that it raises falls;
All whom it may have helped in the past, it will harm.
The soul's in love with it, the eye's fixed on it,
Because of the outward beauty it displays.
God created it to distinguish between
Two groups of mankind: the foolish, and the wise.

21: Imam Ḥabīb ʿAbd Allāh ibn ʿAlawī al-Ḥaddād (d. 1132/1720) was a renowned and influential scholar of Tarīm, Yemen.

يذهب الناس وتخلوا الديارُ
إنمـا الدنيـا بـلاغ لـقوم
هو في أيديهم مستعارُ
فاعـلمنْ واستيقـنن أنّـهُ لا
بد يوما أن يُرَدَّ المُـعارُ

ويقول الإمامُ قطبُ الإرشاد عبد الله بن علوي الحداد رضي الله عنه:

فيم الركون إلى دارٍ حقيقتها
كالطيفِ في سنةٍ والظلّ من مُزَنِ
الزور ظاهِرُها، والغدرُ حاضرها
والموتُ آخرها والكون في الشَّطَنِ
تبيدُ ما جَمَعَتْ، تُهينُ مَن رَفَعَت
تضرُّ مَنْ نَفَعَت في سالفِ الزمن
النفسُ تعشَقُهَا، والعين تـرمُقُها
لكون ظاهرها في صورةِ الحَسَـنِ
إن الإله بـراها كي يَمِيزَ بها
بين الفريقين أهلِ الحُمـقِ والفِطَنِ

Parable 15: An Apt Comparison

Sūrat Hūd (11), Verse 24

The likeness of the two parties is as one who is blind and deaf, and one who can see and hear. Are they equal when compared? Will you not then be mindful?

This verse depicts the condition of the party of the unbelievers and the party of the believers, likening the former to the condition of one who is blind and deaf, and the latter to the condition of one who sees and hears. This is a simple parable rather than a compound one. The first party, namely the unbelievers, do not benefit from examining the clear proofs of God's Oneness in the cosmos and His signs which are visible to all who have eyes. They are like a blind man, who cannot benefit from light and is deprived of the ability to enjoy the diversity of forms and colors. Likewise, the way they do not benefit from the unanswerable proofs of the Qur'ān or the comprehensive call of the Messenger, resembles the condition of a deaf person who does not benefit from sounds and cannot tell pleasant ones from unpleasant ones. The second party, namely the believers, are the opposite: their condition resembles that of someone with good sight and hearing, guided aright by his faculties and blessed with fully functional senses.

Other subtleties of this verse include:

(1) The verse features a rhetorical device called *laff wa nashr*

المثلُ الخامسِ عَشَر: مقارنةٌ سائغةٌ
سورةُ هود الآية (٢٤)

﴿ مَثَلُ الْفَرِيقَيْنِ كَالْأَعْمَى وَالْأَصَمِّ وَالْبَصِيرِ وَالسَّمِيعِ هَلْ يَسْتَوِيَانِ مَثَلًا أَفَلَا تَذَكَّرُونَ ﴾

تشتملُ هذه الآية على تشبيهٍ لحال فريق الكفار وفريقِ المؤمنين بحال الأعمى والأصمِّ من جهةِ الأولِ وحال البصير والسميع من جهة الفريق الثاني وهو تشبيهٌ مفردٌ لا مركب. أما الفريقُ الأول، أعني فريق الكفار فحالهم في عدم الانتفاع بالنظر في دلائل وحدانية الله الواضحة في الكون وآياته المبثوثةِ لكل ذي عين يشبه حال الأعمى في عدم انتفاعه بالضوء وحرمانه من التمتع بشتى الصور والألوان وحالهم في عدم الانتفاع بأدلة القرآن الدامغة ودعوة الرسول البليغة يشبه حال الأصم الذي لا ينتفع بالأصوات ولا يستطيع أن يميز عذبها من منكرها. وأما الفريق الثاني أعني فريق المؤمنين فهم ضد ذلك إذ إن حالهم يشبه سليم البصر سليم السمع، في يقين وهدى من مُدركاته وسلامة تامة في حواسه.

وفي الآية عدا ما سبق لطائف نجمل بعضها فيما يلي:

(folding and unfolding). In this device, more than one thing is mentioned in detail or in general, and then something is said about each of them respectively without specifying which of them is meant, entrusting the hearer with matching them up. In this verse, the way it is used is that the blind and the deaf are mentioned first, each referring to one of the two subjects of the comparison; and then when He says, *and one who can see and hear*, this refers to the other subject of the comparison, which is the "unfolding" after the "folding."

(2) The verse alerts us to the disease as well as the cure, and so our Glorious Lord closes it by saying, *Will you not then be mindful?*—implying that it is possible to cure this blindness and deafness, and that the intelligent person ought to strive as best he can to do so.

(3) The Qur'ān very often castigates those who were tested by possessing hearing and sight but failed to benefit from them. What will a person with two good eyes say on the Day of Resurrection when he is raised up blind and cast into Hell? Will his regret be of any use to him, after he refused to heed the warning? The value of an instrument lies in how it is used; otherwise, it might as well not exist at all, and it will only bring regret.

(١) في الآية لَفٌّ ونَشرٌ واللف والنشر هو ذكر متعدد على التفصيل أو الإجمال ثم ذكر ما لكلٍ من غير تعيينٍ ثقة بأنَّ السامعَ يرده إليه. وهو في الآية حيث عطف الأصم على الأعمى عطف أحد المشبهين على الآخر ثم جاء بقوله **(والبصير والسميع)** فالواو في البصير لعطف التشبيه الثاني على الأول وهو النشر بعد اللفِّ.

(٢) أن الآية قد نَبَّهَت عَلى المرضِ والعلاجِ فَخَتَمَها ربُّنا سبحانهُ بقولهِ **(أفلا تَذَكَّرُونَ)** منبها على أن علاج العمى والصمم ممكنٌ ولذا يجب على العاقل أن يسعى في ذلك قدر الإمكان.

(٣) قلتُ: وكم شَنَّعَ القرآنُ عَلى أولئكَ الذينَ ابتُلُوا بالسمع والبصر فما وُفِّقوا للانتفاعِ بِهِمَا. وَمَا يقولُ صاحبُ العينينِ يومَ القيامةِ حِيَن يُحشَرُ أعمى، وفي جهنم يُرمى؟ أينفعهُ الندمُ بعدَ أنْ تَصامَمَ عَنِ النَّذيرِ؟ إن قيمةَ الآلاتِ في حصولِ الانفعالاتِ وإلا فهي كالعدمِ وسببُ كلِّ نَدَمٍ.

Parable 16: Holding On to Water

Sūrat al-Raʿd (13), Verse 14

Those upon whom they call apart from Him cannot give them any answer, but only as one who stretches out his hands to water so that it may reach his mouth, though it will never reach it. The calls of the disbelievers are simply in vain.

This parable depicts the state of the idol-worshipers who make requests of their companions and their gods but do not receive anything. It likens them to a thirsty person who scoops up water in his open palms instead of cupping them and tries to lift it to his mouth to drink, but nothing reaches his mouth because the water will not stay in his hands, and so his efforts are utterly wasted. This image and parable were well-known to the Arabs, who would say when someone made an effort in vain, "He may as well try to hold onto water." They viewed this as a sign of foolishness and futility. Abū ʿUbayda[22] said:

> I became, in the love between me and her,
> Like someone trying to grasp water in his hand.

Another poet said:

22: Abū ʿUbayda Maʿmar ibn al-Muthannā (d. 209/825) was an influential Persian grammarian of the Arabic language.

المثلُ السادس عَشَر: القابض على الماء
سورةُ الرعد الآية (١٤)

﴿وَالَّذِينَ يَدْعُونَ مِنْ دُونِهِ لَا يَسْتَجِيبُونَ لَهُمْ بِشَيْءٍ إِلَّا كَبَاسِطِ كَفَّيْهِ إِلَى الْمَاءِ لِيَبْلُغَ فَاهُ وَمَا هُوَ بِبَالِغِهِ وَمَا دُعَاءُ الْكَافِرِينَ إِلَّا فِي ضَلَالٍ﴾

شبه هيئة عباد الأصنام وهم يطلبون من أصحابهم وآلهتهم فلا ينالون شيئا بحال الظمآن الذي يغترف الماء بكفين مبسوطتين غير مقبوضتين ويريد أن يرفعه لفمه ليروى فلا ينال من ذلك شيئا إذ لا يستقر الماء فيهما فيبوء جهده بالبوار ويذهب سعيه وتعبه سدى. وهذه الصورة وهذا المثل معروفان عند العرب حيث يقولون لمن يطلب ما لا يحصل له: (هو كالقابض على الماء) ويرون ذلك علامة على الحمق والخيبة التامة. قال أبو عبيدة:

فأصبحتُ فِيمَا كانَ بَيْنِي وَبَيْنَهَا
مِن الوُدِّ مثلَ القَابِضِ الماءَ بِاليَدِ

وقال الشاعر:

فأَصبَحْتُ مِنْ ليْلى الغَدَاةَ كَقَابِضٍ
على الماءِ خَانَتْهُ فُرُوجُ الأَصَابِعِ

With Laylā this morning, I've became like someone
Who tries to hold water running through his fingers.

Other lessons of this verse include:

(1) It corresponds to other parables which the Arabs would use to depict foolishness and futility. For example, they used to say, "He is more stupid than a water-lapper," "more fatheaded than a water-chewer," "more foolish than a water-grasper," or "more silly than a water-licker." By this they meant to portray someone so foolish that he would attempt to chew or lick water rather than drink it.

(2) It is said that the parable portrays the attachment of those deluded people to the gods they worship instead of God, despite not being answered by them, by likening them to a thirsty person who stretches out his hands to water that is out of reach down at the bottom of a well, hoping that the water will respond to his hands and rise up to his mouth, which of course it will never do. This is a tangible image which the mind can visualize so clearly that the eyes can almost see it. The verse contains a metonym for futile hopes. Metonym (*kināya*), according to experts in rhetoric, means a way of expressing something by referring to it indirectly for one purpose or another: for instance, we might say an innocent person has "clean hands" or that a talkative person is "long-winded", and so on.[23]

(3) The use of the preposition "in" at the end of the verse is guaranteed to inspire the heart of the listener and the reader to imagine the distance of those people whose calls have been utterly squandered. The restrictive term "simply" is then used, adding further beauty to the expression.

23: The Arabic examples given by the author here are *ṭāhir al-dhayl* (clean-hemmed) for a chaste person, and *ṭawīl al-lisān* (long-tongued) for a talkative person.

ومما يتَعَلَّقُ بهذهِ الآيةِ من المَعَاني:

(١) أَنَّها تتوافَقُ مع الأَمثَالِ التي تضربها العرب في الحُمقِ وخيبةِ الأملِ ومنها قولهم: "أَحمَقُ مِنْ لاعِقِ الماءِ" وقولهم: "أحمقُ من مَاضِغِ المَاءِ" و قولهم: "أَحمَقُ من القَابِضِ على الماءِ" وقولهم: "أَحْمَقُ من مَاطِخِ المَاءِ" وماطخُ الماءِ هو الذي لا يُحسنُ شربه من حُمقِهِ ولكن يلْعَقُهُ. ومعنى قولهم: "أَحْمَقُ مِن.." أي غاية ما يُتصوَّرُ في الحُمقِ من يقبض على الماء أو يمضُغُه او يلعَقُهُ.

(٢) قِيلَ إِنّ التَّصوِيرَ هُنَا لِاستمرارِ تَعَلُّقِ هؤلاءِ المَغْرُورِينَ بآلِهَتِهِم التي يَعبُدُونَها مِن دونِ اللهِ معَ عَدَم حصول الاستجابة بحالِ ظَمآنٍ راحَ يبْسُطُ كَفَّيهِ نحوَ ماءٍ بعيدٍ يلْمَعُ في قاعِ بئْرٍ ليستَجيبَ الماء لكفَّيْهِ ويَرْتَفِعَ فَيبلُغَ فاه؛ وأنَّى له أن يبلُغْ؟ فهي صورة متخليةٌ محسوسَةٌ تكادُ تَرَاها العيونُ. وفي الآية كنايةٌ عن خيبةِ الداعي. والكناية - عند علماء البيان- هي التعبير عن شيءٍ بلفظٍ غيرِ صريح في الدلالةِ عليه لغَرضٍ من الأغراضِ مثل أن نعبر عن عفة إنسان بأن نقول "طاهر الذيل" أو عن سلاطته بأن نقول: "طويل اللسان"...الخ.

(٣) أَنَّهُ استخدمَ حرفَ الجَرّ "في" فى آخرِ الآيةِ وهو كَفيلٌ بأَنِ يأخُذَ بقلبِ السامعِ والقارئِ إلى تَخَيُّلٍ بعيد لِأولئك الذين ذهب دعاءهم في دروبِ الضياع، ثم استخدمَ أُسلُوبَ القَصْرِ ليزيدَ التَعْبيرَ جَمالاً على جمالِهِ.

Parable 17: The Likeness of Truth and Falsehood

Sūrat al-Raʿd (13), Verse 17

He sends down water from the sky so that the riverbeds flow according to their capacity, and the torrent carries a scum that swells; and from that which they smelt in the fire, desiring ornaments or utensils, there is a scum like it. Thus does God set forth truth and falsehood. As for the scum, it disappears as dross, while that which is of use to people remains in the earth. Thus does God set forth parables.

This verse features two comparisons. In the first, God the Exalted and Glorious depicts truth, meaning knowledge of God and His teachings, and its benefit and power when it reaches ears and hearts, likening it to a great quantity of rain which falls from the sky and flows through the riverbeds. He likens the hearts in which this truth settles, and which absorb it in their differing levels, to the riverbeds, each of which takes as much as it can hold. Then He likens the falsehood which this truth destroys and dispels, and all of the doubts which are attached to it, to the scum that visibly swells up on the surface of the water but contains no benefit, and disappears leaving the pure water for people to benefit from.

In the second comparison, God likens the truth to the substances which people smelt in fire, such as gold, silver, and other metals, in order to make ornaments and utensils to benefit from; and He likens falsehood to the dross which is expelled during the smelting process,

المثلُ السابعَ عَشَر: مثال الحق والباطل
سورةُ الرعد الآية (١٧)

﴿أَنْزَلَ مِنَ السَّمَاءِ مَاءً فَسَالَتْ أَوْدِيَةٌ بِقَدَرِهَا فَاحْتَمَلَ السَّيْلُ زَبَدًا رَابِيًا وَمِمَّا يُوقِدُونَ عَلَيْهِ فِي النَّارِ ابْتِغَاءَ حِلْيَةٍ أَوْ مَتَاعٍ زَبَدٌ مِثْلُهُ كَذَلِكَ يَضْرِبُ اللَّهُ الْحَقَّ وَالْبَاطِلَ فَأَمَّا الزَّبَدُ فَيَذْهَبُ جُفَاءً وَأَمَّا مَا يَنْفَعُ النَّاسَ فَيَمْكُثُ فِي الْأَرْضِ كَذَلِكَ يَضْرِبُ اللَّهُ الْأَمْثَالَ﴾

تحتوي هذه الآيةُ على تشبيهين أولهما: أنّه - سبحانه وتعالى- شبّه الحق - وهو العلمُ بالله وأحكامه- في إفادته وثباته ونفعه حين يردُ على الأَسماعِ والقلوبِ بالماءِ الكثير النازلِ من السَّماءِ فتسيلُ به الأدوية ومثَّل القلوبَ التي سكنَ فيها ووَعَتْ عنه على اختلافِ مراتِبِها بالأَوْدِيَةِ -كلٌّ يحْمِلُ على قدره- وشبّه الباطِلَ الذي دَمَغَهُ ذلك الحقَّ وذَهبَ به وما تعلَّق به من شبهاتٍ بالزَّبَدِ المُنتَفِخِ في صورته الظاهر فوق الماء لكنه لا نفعَ فيه يذهبُ ويبقى الماءُ الخالصُ الصافي لينتَفِعَ به الناسُ.

والتشبيه الثاني: شبَّه فيه الحقَّ بما يصْهَرُهُ النَّاسُ من ذَهَبٍ وفضةٍ وغيرها من المعادنِ ليتخذوا منه حليا ومتاعا

having hitherto adulterated those metals. It is then thrown away into the fire, since it is useless, while the original metal remains to be used. The call to truth, then, is like fire which separates the beneficial from the harmful, the lean from the fat.

Other lessons of the verse include:

(1) It combines two comparisons for the benefit of two groups of people. The first are those who live in the countryside, who have witnessed how rivers rise and flow after rainfall and have the image of it in their minds, so that the first parable suits them well. The second are townsfolk, such as the Meccans, who do not see rivers in torrent every day but can see another image: smithing for jewelry and tools. The second parable is for them, depicting the concept in a manner familiar to them.

(2) The verse depicts two types of hearts and the way they react to Revelation. There are hearts in which faith settles with a powerful impact, so that they benefit greatly whenever God's Signs and verses pass before them. They have differing levels in this benefit, since benefit is commensurate with elevation. Other hearts are proud and scornful, always seeking what is foul, and so they experience neither benefit nor elevation.

(3) Regarding His words *Thus does God set forth parables*, [the word] *ka-dhālika* (thus) reminds one of] the word *fadhlaka*, which means "conclusion", as in the conclusion of a parable. It is derived from how mathematicians say, "therefore, that was thus" (*fa-dhālika kān kadhā*) by way of introducing the result of a mathematical operation. The word *fadhlaka* then came to be used to refer to any kind of result derived from a process, whether mathematical or otherwise. It is a portmanteau word, like *basmala* (saying *Bism Allāh*, "in the Name of God"), *ḥamdala* (saying *al-Ḥamd li-Llāh*, "praise be to God"), and other [shortened compounds of two words].

ينتفعون به وشبَّهَ الباطِلَ بالخَبَثِ الذي يُقذَفُ أثناء عملية الصهر مما قد يكون قد اختلطَ بتلك المعادن فتلقي به النار بعيدا لعدم صلاحه لشيءٍ بينما يُستَبقى المعدنُ الأصيل النافعُ لُيستَخدَم. وكأنَّ عملية الدعوة بمثابة نار تفصل النافع من الضار والغثَّ من السمين.

وفي الآيةِ فوائد مُنْها:

(١) أنّها جَمَعَت تَشبِيهَينِ لإفادةِ فريقين من الناس؛ الفريق الأول هم أهل البوادي ممن لهم اطلاعٌ على الأودية وسيلانها بالماء وصورةُ ذلك حاضرة في عقولهم فناسبهم التشبيه الأول، والفريق الثاني هم أهل الحواضر - كأهلِ مَكَّةَ- ممن لا يُشاهدونَ سيولَ الأودية كل يوم لكن يرون صورةً أخرى وهي صهرُ الحليّ والمعادنِ فضربَ لَهُم المثل الثاني تقريبا للمعنى بما يشاهدون.

(٢) أنَّ الآيةَ أَفَادَتْ عن نوعين من القلوبِ في تعاملهما مع الوحيِ؛ قلوبٌ استقر فيها الإيمان بقوة فتنتفع أيما انتفاع حين تمرُّ عليها الآيات وهي على مراتب في هذا الانتفاع إذ الانتفاع على قدرِ الارتفاع، وأخرى مستكبرة منكرة تطلب الخبيث فلا تنتفع ولا ترتفع.

(٣) قوله: **(كذلك يضرب الله الأمثال)** فذلكةُ التمثيل أي نتيجته وكلمة فذلكة مأخوذة من قول الحُسّابِ "فذلك كان كذا" فذلك إشارة إلى الحساب ونتيجته ثم اطلقت كلمة **(الفذلكة)** لكل ما هو نتيجة متفرعة على ما سبق حسابا كان أو غير ذلك. وهي كلمةٌ مركبةٌ مثل: بسملة، و حمدله وغيرها.

Parable 18: The Good Word and the Bad Word

Sūrat Ibrāhīm (14), Verses 24-26

Have you not seen how God sets forth a parable? A goodly word is like a goodly tree, its root set firm and its branches in heaven. It brings forth fruit in every season, by the leave of its Lord. God sets forth parables for mankind, that they might be mindful. And the likeness of a bad word is as a bad tree, uprooted from the face of the earth, having no stability.

In these verses God sets forth a parable for a word [or saying] of faith and a word [or saying] of unbelief and the external and internal effects associated with each, likening them to the state of two trees. The first—the word of Islam, which is the testimony that there is no god but God, and that Muḥammad is His Servant and Messenger—is depicted with reference to its outcomes, which are splendor on the sensory plane, joy in the soul, and successive benefits for anyone who holds to it. This is achieved by comparing it to a tree with firm roots, a pleasing appearance, and ample delicious fruits.

The second—the word of unbelief—is also depicted with reference to its outcomes, which are doctrinal confusion, conceptual turmoil, anxiety, and repeated harm. This is achieved by comparing it to a bad tree lacking roots and stability, possessing no benefit but only futility and ruin. The purpose is to depict each state individually.

Other subtleties and secrets of these verses include:

(1) The good tree is described as having four attributes: [i] It

المثلُ الثامِنْ عَشَر: (الكلمة الطيبة والكلمة الخبيثة) سورةُ إبراهيم الآيات (٢٤-٢٦)

﴿أَلَمْ تَرَ كَيْفَ ضَرَبَ اللَّهُ مَثَلًا كَلِمَةً طَيِّبَةً كَشَجَرَةٍ طَيِّبَةٍ أَصْلُهَا ثَابِتٌ وَفَرْعُهَا فِي السَّمَاءِ تُؤْتِي أُكُلَهَا كُلَّ حِينٍ بِإِذْنِ رَبِّهَا وَيَضْرِبُ اللَّهُ الْأَمْثَالَ لِلنَّاسِ لَعَلَّهُمْ يَتَذَكَّرُونَ وَمَثَلُ كَلِمَةٍ خَبِيثَةٍ كَشَجَرَةٍ خَبِيثَةٍ اجْتُثَّتْ مِنْ فَوْقِ الْأَرْضِ مَا لَهَا مِنْ قَرَارٍ﴾

ضرب الله في هذه الآيات مثلا لكلمةِ الإيمان وكلمة الكفر وما يتَرَتَّبُ على كلٍ واحدةٍ منهما من آثار ظاهرة وباطنة بحال شجرتين فالأولى- أعني كلمة الإسلام وهي شهادة أن لا إله إلا الله وأن محمدً عبده ورسوله- تشبه في هيئة ما يحصلُ عنها من بهجةٍ في الحس، وفرحٍ في النَّفس وحصول المنافع المتتالية لصاحبها بهيئة شجرةٍ راسخةِ الأصل، بهية المنظر، وافرةِ الثمارِ، لذيذة المأكل. والثانية - أعني كلمة الكفر- تشبه -في هيئة ما ينشأ عنها من اضطراب في الاعتقاد، وتخبطٍ في التصورات، وضيق في الصدر، وضرٍّ مُتعَاقِبٍ- شجرةً خبيثةً لا أصل لها ولا قرار، ولا نفع فيها بل كلّها بوار. والغرضُ تمثيل كل حالةٍ على حدة.

وفي الآيات لطائف خفية وأسرار جليلة منها:

is goodly (*ṭayyiba*), which is inclusive of its appearance, its scent, its fruits, and their flavor. [ii] It is firmly-rooted and stable, never wilting or dying, which evokes a sense of security. [iii] Its branches are in heaven, which indicates that it is in a state of perfection, free of all blights. [iv] It gives forth fruit all the time, which indicates that it yields copious pleasure without interruption. There is no doubt that knowledge of God Most High and immersion in His love resembles such a tree in all of those ways. There is nothing better or more fitting for a human being than it; nor anything firmer or more stable for the soul; nor anything more perfect than its branches, which connect with God and bring His servants kindness and compassion; nor anything more enduring than its fruits, whose effects are present at all times, heralding the achievement of every perfection.

(2) The bad tree is described as having three attributes: [i] it is bad; [ii] it has no roots; [iii] it has no stability. Likewise, unbelief in God and ignorance of Him is foul is appearance and scent, containing many harms, and has no arguments or strength to support it. Note that listing three attributes for the bad tree, but four for the good, evokes the lowliness of the bad tree even in the very number of its qualities.

(3) God's Words *by the leave of its Lord* contain a subtle detail alluding to how any good thing which emerges from God's servant, and any virtuous state which he enters, has its origin and source entirely in the Glorious Lord. The believer ought to ascend from exulting in states, which come from the Lord, to exulting in the Lord Himself. One of the people of true realization said, "Whoever prefers knowledge for knowledge's sake has affirmed the existence of that which shall perish (*fānī*).[24] Whoever prefers knowledge not for its own sake, but for the Known, has plunged boldly into the depths of the sea of attainment."

24: The original quotation from Ibn Sīnā's *Ishārāt*, as quoted by al-Rāzī and others, has "affirmed the existence of the second (*al-thānī*)", i.e., a second God.

(١) أنَّ الشجرةَ الطيِّبةَ وُصِفَت بصفاتٍ أربعٍ وهي [١] كونها طيبة وذلك يشمل الصورة والرائحة والثمرة واللذة الناشئة من أكلها [٢] وكونها ثابتة الأصل راسخة لا تنقضي ولا تنقرض وهو باعث على الاطمئنان [٣] وكون فرعها في السماء وهو دالٌّ على كمال الحال والتنزه عن العفوناتِ [٤] وكونُ أُكُلِها حاضر في كل الأوقات وهو دالٌّ على وفور اللذة وعدم الانقطاع. ولاشكَّ أنَّ معرفة الله تعالى والاستغراق في محبته تشبه تلك الشجرة من هذه الوجوه كلِّها فلا أطيب ولا أنسبَ للمرء منها، ولا أثبت ولا أرسخ في النفس ولا أكمل منها في الفرع إذ تتصل فروعها بالله وتعود آثارها على خلقه شفقةً وحنانا ولا أدومَ من أكلها وثمارها لأن آثارها حاضرة في كل حال ومؤذن بحصول كلِّ كمال.

(٢) أنَّ الشجرةَ الخبيثة وُصفت بصفاتٍ ثلاث وهي [١] كونها خبيثة [٢] ولا أصل لها ولا عرق [٣] ولا قرار لها. وكذلك الكفر بالله والجهل به خبيث المنظر والريح، مشتمل على المضار الكثيرة، لا حجةَ له ولا ثبات ولا قوة. قلت: وفي وصف الخبيثة بثلاث صفات مع وصف الطيبة بأربع إظهار لدونية الخبيثة حتى في عدد صفاتها.

(٣) في قوله تعالى (**بإذن ربها**) دقيقة تشير إلى أنَّ كلَّ خير يصدر من العبد وكلَّ حال سنيٍّ يتلبس به إنما أساسه ومصدره من المولى سبحانه فعلى المؤمن أن يترقى من الفرح بالأحوال التي هي من المَوْلى إلى الفرح بالمولى. قال بعضُ المحققين: من آثر العرفان للعرفان فقد قال بالفاني، ومَن آثر العرفان لا

(4) One scholar commented on this parable that "The reason God Most High compared faith to a tree is that a tree is not worthy of being called a tree unless it has three things: firm roots, an upright trunk, and high branches; and likewise, faith is not complete unless it has three things: knowledge in the heart, affirmation with the tongue, and actions with the body." I would add that this can also be gleaned from the expression in *Sūrat al-Raḥmān* when God Most High says, *And the herbs and the trees* [Qur'ān 55:6], calling what grows from the earth without a trunk a "herb", and what grows from it upon a trunk a "tree." It has been said that the "good tree" is the date palm, and the bad tree is the colocynth, but that is a [matter of] lengthy debate and there is no reason to specify any particular kind. The good tree described in the verse is noble, whether it is one which exists in the world or not.

للعرفان بل للمعروف فقد خاضَ لُجَّة الوصول.

(٤) قال بعضُ العلماءِ في تقريرِ هذا المثلِ: إِنّمَا مثَّل الله تعالى الإيمان بالشجرة لأن الشجرة لا تستحق أن تسمى شجرة إلا بثلاثة أشياء؛ عرقٌ راسخ وأصلٌ قائم وأغصانٌ عالية، كذلك الإيمان لا يتم إلا بثلاثة أشياء، معرفة في القلب، وقول باللسان وعمل بالأبدان. ا.هـ. قلت: ويستفاد هذا من العطف في سورة الرحمن حيث قال الله تعالى: **(والنجمُ والشجر)** فسمى ما ينجم من الأرض مما لا ساق له نجما وما يخرج منها وله ساق **(شجرا)**. وقيل في الشجرة الطيبة أنها النخلة وفي الخبيثة أنها الحنظل وهو كلام يطول ولا حاجة لتحديد واحدةٍ فإن الشجرة الطيبة المشار إليها شريفة سواءً كان لها وجود دنيوي أم لا.

Parable 19: The Powerless Idols

Sūrat al-Naḥl (16), Verse 75

God sets forth a parable: a slave who is a chattel, having no power over anything, and one whom We have given a fair provision from Us, from which he spends secretly and openly. Are they equal? Praise be to God! But most of them know not.

This verse compares the state of idols taken as objects of worship besides God to the state of a slave who has no power over his own person and owns no possessions. God the Exalted also compares the provision He grants to all His servants to the state of a rich man who is in control of his own affairs and may choose whether or not to spend of his wealth. The purpose of this parable is to rebuke the unbelievers for likening God to His creation or likening His creation to Him.

Reason attests to the simple fact that there can be no equivalence between the state of the powerless slave and the powerful master, so how could any rational person allow an equivalence between the All-Powerful God Most High and idols which have no power or possessions at all?

It has also been said that the purpose of this comparison is to liken the unbeliever, who refuses to worship and obey God, to the chattel slave, who is powerless, humiliated, and impoverished; and to liken the believer, who fulfils his duty of reverence to God and his duty of good conduct and compassion to his fellow man, to the

المثلُ التاسع عَشَر: الأصنام العاجزة
سورة النحل الآية (٧٥)

﴿ ضَرَبَ اللَّهُ مَثَلًا عَبْدًا مَمْلُوكًا لَا يَقْدِرُ عَلَى شَيْءٍ وَمَنْ رَزَقْنَاهُ مِنَّا رِزْقًا حَسَنًا فَهُوَ يُنْفِقُ مِنْهُ سِرًّا وَجَهْرًا هَلْ يَسْتَوُونَ الْحَمْدُ لِلَّهِ بَلْ أَكْثَرُهُمْ لَا يَعْلَمُونَ ﴾

شبه في هذه الآية حال الأصنام والمعبودات المُتَّخذَةَ مِنْ دونِ الله بحالِ مملوكٍ لا يقدِرُ على تصرُّفٍ في نفسِهِ ولا يملِكُ مالاً وشبَّهَ شَأْنَ الله تعالى في رزقه لعباده أجمعين بحال الغنيِّ المالِكِ أمرَ نفسهِ بما شاء من إنفاق وغيره. والغرضُ من هذا التمثيل زجرهم (أي الكفار) عن أن يُشَبِّهوا الله تعالى بخلقه أو أن يشبهوا الخلق بربهم فصريح.

العقل يشهدُ بأنه لا يجوز التسويةُ بين حال العبد العاجزِ والحر القادرِ، فكيفَ يجوزُ لعاقلٍ أن يُسَويَ بين الله تعالى القادرِ وبين الأصنامِ التي لا تملِكُ ولا تقدرُ على شيءٍ البتةَ.

وقيل إنَّ التشبيهَ المقصود به تشبيه الكافر في حرمانه من عبودية الله تعالى وطاعته بالعبد المملوك العاجز الذليل الفقير وتشبيه المؤمن المُشتَغل بحقوق الله من تعظيم وحقوق

free man, who is noble and able and who gives charity secretly and openly.

But the first interpretation is better and more plausible, because the verse is situated in the context of affirming God's Oneness and refuting idol-worship.

Other subtleties of the verse include:

(1) Note that the slave is described as *a chattel, having no power over anything*, even though one might assume those things to be true of any slave. The purpose of this is to differentiate between him and a *mukātab* (conditionally enfranchised) slave, and the slave whose master has allowed him some freedom of action.

(2) The verse is situated after a succession of diverse arguments for God's Oneness, including a recounting of the blessings which none but He can provide such as the blessing of children and grandchildren, and the apportioning of provisions both inward and outward. This verse acts as a sort of complement to that passage, shifting the discourse to rational argument and providing rhetorical diversification which leaves no room for resistance. That is why the verse concludes with the words; *Praise be to God!* That is, "Praise be to God for the clarity and power of this argument."

(3) Addendum. This parable is followed by another in the next verse[25] in which the state of the idolaters' idols and objects of worship is compared to a man who is dumb and powerless and cannot defend or benefit himself, and is nothing but a burden to his master. God the Glorious then compares Himself to someone who enjoins justice, which requires speech, power, and knowledge. The object of this parable, as with the one which precedes it, is to chastise them for equating their inert lifeless idols with the True Lord, and to vividly

25: *And God sets forth a parable: two men, one of whom is dumb, having no power over anything, a burden to his master; wherever he dispatches him, he brings no good. Is he equal to one who enjoins justice and follows a straight path?* [Qur'ān 16:76]

النَّاس من حُسنِ مُعَامَلَةٍ وشَفَقَةٍ بالحُرّ الكريم القادِرِ المُنْفِقِ سِرّاً وجَهرا. والقولُ الأولُ أقربُ وأولَى لأنَّ الآية وردت في سياق إثباتِ التوحيدِ وإبطالِ عبادةِ الأصنامِ.

وفي الآية لطائف منها:

(١) أنَّ وصف العبد بكونه **(مملوك)** و **(لا يقدرُ على شيء)** مع كونِ العبد في الأصلِ مملوك ولا يملكُ التصرفَ، الغرضُ منه التمييز بينه وبين المكاتب والمأذونِ له في التَّصرفِ.

(٢) أنَّ الآية وردت بعد تقريرِ أَنواعٍ كثيرةٍ من دلائلِ التوحيد كتعدادِ النعم التي لا يقومُ بها سواه كنعمة البنين والأحفاد، وتقسيم الأرزاق الباطنة والظاهرة، فكانت هذه الآية بمثابة إكمالٍ للمشهدِ حيثُ انتقلَت إلى التَّدْلِيلِ العقليّ وهو تنويع في الخطاب لا يَدَعُ مَحَلًّا للإنكارِ ولذلك خُتِمَت الآيةُ بقوله **(الحمدُ لله)** أي الحمدُ لله على ظهور هذه الحُجَّة وقوتها.

(٣) تذييلٌ: ورد بعد هذا المثل مثلُ آخر في الآية التي تليها وتقريره أن الله تعالى شبّهَ حالَ أصنامِهِم ومعبوداتهم بحال رجل أبكم عاجز لا يستطيعُ دَفْعاً ولا نَفْعاً بل هو ثقيل على مولاه، ومَثَّلَ لنفسه سُبحانَهُ بِمَنْ يأمرُ بالعدلِ والأمرُ بالعدلِ يستَلْزِمُ النُّطق والقُدرَةَ والعِلم. والغرضُ من هذا المثل -كسابقه- زَجرَهُم عن التسويةِ بين معبوداتهم الجامدة الخامدة الهامِدَةِ وبين المولى المعبود الحق وتحقيقِ

portray the distinction to them so that they may realize the disparity and be left with no counter-arguments, and to dispel their doubts and leave them with nothing to say and no excuses to proffer. The reason why we have not included that parable in its own section is that it is very close in meaning and purpose to the one preceding it.

صورةِ المُغَايَرَةِ لديهم كي يظهر لهم التفاوُتُ فتنقطع حججهم وترتفعَ شُبَهُهُم ولا يبقى لهم قولٌ ولا عذر. وإنما لم نورد هذا المثل منفصلا لقربه من سابقه في المعنى والغرض.

Parable 20: Breaking Promises
Sūrat al-Naḥl (16), Verse 92

Do not be like her who unravels her yarn
into strands after it was strong.

This verse compares a person who goes back on his word after giving it, and breaks his oath after swearing it, to a woman who was proverbial among the Arabs as a symbol of treachery and disloyalty, having unraveled her yarn after it was tightly spun. Her name, according to the most prevalent account, was Rīṭa bint Saʿd al-Tamīmiyya, and she was from the Tamīm clan of Quraysh. The Qur'ān does not mention her by name, either because the Arabs knew her better by that description, or simply in accordance with the usual Qur'ānic practice of not mentioning people by name unless they were known for a particular thing.

The story of that woman states that she was a madwoman who had several maids. She had a spinning-mill and a huge spindle, and she and her maids would spin from dawn until noon, whereupon she would order them to unravel all that they had spun. She would repeat that cycle every day. She became known as a paragon of the pointless destruction of something beneficial and well-done, and people would say, "He is madder than the woman who unraveled her yarn!"

She is likened here to a person who goes back on their oath, because oaths ought to be honored, just as the effort taken to spin

المثلُ العشرون: الخُلفُ بالوَعد
سورةُ النحل الآية (٩٢)

﴿ وَلَا تَكُونُوا كَالَّتِي نَقَضَتْ غَزْلَهَا مِنْ بَعْدِ قُوَّةٍ أَنْكَاثًا ﴾

في هذه الآيةِ تشبيهٌ للذي يرجعُ في يَمِينهِ بعد إحكامِهِ وينقُضُ عَهْدَهُ بعد عَقْدِهِ بامرأةٍ كانت العربُ تضرب بها المثل في الخيبةِ والخَرَق- حيث كانت تنقُضُ غَزْلَهَا بعد شدةِ فَتْلِهِ. واسمُ هذه المرأةِ على الأشهرِ ريطةُ بنت سعد التميمية من بني تميم من قريش. ولم يذكُرها القرآن باسمها لأن العربَ كانوا يعرفُونَهَا بِوَصفِها ذاك أو على عادةِ القرآن في الستر حيث لم يذكُرْ بالاسم العَلمِ إلا مَن اشتهر بأمر مُعَيّنٍ.

وجاءَ في قصة تلك المرأةِ أنها كانت خرقاء مختلّةَ العقل لها جوارٍ وقد اتخذت مغزلا وفلكةً ضخمةً فكانت تغزِلُ هي وجواريها من الغداةِ إلى الظهر ثم تأمرهنَّ فينقضنَ وتنقضُ ما غزلنَ وتفعلُ هذا كلَّ يومٍ فضُربَ بها المثل في إفسادِ ما كانَ نافعاً مُحكماً وقيل: أخرق من ناكثةٍ غزلها.

وشُبّهَ بها مَنْ يعودُ في يمينه لأن الأيمان تستحقُ التعظيم، كما أَنَّ الجهد المبذول في الغزل يستحقُ العناية والاهتمام. وإفسادُ الأيمان يؤدي للخصام والعداوة فشنعَ

yarn ought to be respected and valued. Breaking an oath leads to enmity and rivalry, and so the Qur'ān castigates those who do it by comparing them to the act of Rīṭa the madwoman.

Other lessons of the verse include:

(1) It forbids returning from faith to unbelief, because the covenant of faith deserves loyalty above all others. The verse does not say that they actually broke their oaths, but only warns them not to.

(2) Describing the yarn as strong implies that there was no reason for unraveling it. Were it not described as strong, one might imagine that the yarn was not spun well and that it was unraveled for a good reason, but this description entirely discounts that possibility.

(3) The parable indicates that it is a kind of oath-breaking to perform one's acts of worship while neglecting the good conduct and behavior that ought to accompany them. Good deeds require certain attitudes, and if one performs them without those attitudes, his deeds are at risk of lacking sincerity or even being invalid. For example, if a person prays and fasts but then hurts other people with his words or actions, then his prayer and fasting will be fruitless.

There are several hadiths about this, including the one narrated by Imam Bukhārī in *al-Adab al-mufrad* on the authority of Abū Hurayra ﵁, who related that someone asked the Prophet ﷺ, "Messenger of God, So-and-So prays through the night and fasts through the day, and works, and gives charity, but she hurts her neighbors with her words." The Messenger of God ﷺ replied, "There is no good in her, and she is one of the people of Hell." They said, "What about So-and-So, who prays the five prayers, and gives bits of cheese for charity, but does not hurt anyone?" The Messenger of God ﷺ replied, "She is one of the people of Paradise."[26]

26: *Al-Adab al-mufrad* 119.

القرآن على فاعليه بتشبيه فعلهم بفعل ريطة الخرقاء.
ومن المعاني المستفادةِ من الآية:

(١) النهي عن الرجوع من الإيمان إلى الكفر إذ إنَّ عهد الإيمان أولى بالوفاء. ولا تقتضي الآية وقوع النقض بالفعل فيهم بل غاية ما فيها التحذير.

(٢) في نسبة القوةِ للغزل إشعار بعدم وجود سبب موجب للنقض، إذ لو لم يوصف الغزل بالقوة لورد عليه أن يكون غزلا غير مُحكَمٍ فيكون نقضه لإصلاحه فنفى ذلك تماما بذلك الوصف.

(٣) التنبيه على أن من صور نقض الأيمانِ أن لا يقوم الإنسان بما يتوجب على العبادات من حُسنِ معاملة وسلوك، إذ إن الأعمال تستوجبُ أحوالا فمنْ لم تظهَرْ عليهِ تلك الأحوال، يُخْشى عليه من خلوِ أعماله من صدق التوجه بل يكون ناقضا لها. وذلك مثل من يصلي ويصوم ثمَّ يؤذي الناسِ بلسانه أو يده، فلا ثمرة لصيامه أو صلاته. وقد وردت الأحاديث حول هذا المعنى منها ما رواه الإمام البخاري في الأدب المُفردِ من حديث أبي هريرة رضي الله عنه: "قِيلَ لِلنَّبِيِّ صلى الله عليه وسلم: يَا رَسُولَ اللَّهِ، إِنَّ فُلاَنَةَ تَقُومُ اللَّيْلَ وَتَصُومُ النَّهَارَ، وَتَفْعَلُ، وَتَصَّدَّقُ، وَتُؤْذِي جِيرَانَهَا بِلِسَانِهَا؟ فَقَالَ رَسُولُ اللَّهِ صلى الله عليه وسلم: لاَ خَيْرَ فِيهَا، هِيَ مِنْ أَهْلِ النَّارِ، قَالُوا: وَفُلاَنَةُ تُصَلِّي الْمَكْتُوبَةَ، وَتَصَّدَّقُ بِأَثْوَارٍ، وَلاَ تُؤْذِي أَحَدًا؟ فَقَالَ رَسُولُ اللَّهِ صلى الله عليه وسلم: هِيَ مِنْ أَهْلِ الْجَنَّةِ."

Parable 21: The Eternal Value of Deeds

Sūrat al-Isrā' (17), Verse 13

And We have fastened every human's destiny to his neck; and We shall bring forth for him, on the Day of Resurrection, a book he will find laid open.

This verse compares the deeds of a human being—which God always knew that he would do in the world, and to which he would be bound, whether they be good or evil—to a bird of augury (*ṭā'ir*), or a divining arrow to which they would attach feathers so that it resembled a bird. The basis of this comparison is that it was the custom of the Arabs that when they wished to do something and wanted to know whether that course of action would spell good or evil for them, they would scare up a bird. If it flew to the right, they would take it as a good omen; if it flew to the left, they would take it as a bad omen.

Likewise, when they wanted to apportion something or determine someone's share of an award or a division, they would write the names of the parties on arrows and attach feathers to them to make them more aerodynamic. Then they would shoot the arrows at whatever was to be divided up, and each party would get the thing or the piece which his arrow hit. As the feathered arrows flew through the air, they resembled birds.

So here the Qur'ān likens God's pre-eternal decree of the deeds that every person will perform in the world to the birds which they

المثلُ الحادي والعشرون: تقدير الأعمال في الأزل
سورةُ الإسراء الآية (١٣)

﴿ وَكُلَّ إِنْسَانٍ أَلْزَمْنَاهُ طَائِرَهُ فِي عُنُقِهِ وَنُخْرِجُ لَهُ يَوْمَ الْقِيَامَةِ كِتَابًا يَلْقَاهُ مَنْشُورًا ﴾

مَثّلَتْ هَذهِ الآيةُ عَمَلَ الإِنسَانِ - الذي سَبقَ في علمِ اللهُ وقوعَهُ مِنهُ في الدُّنيا ومُلازَمَتَهُ لهُ خيرا كان أو شرا- بالطائر أو بالسهام التي كان يوضع فيها الريش فتكون على هيئة طائر. وأصلُ هذا التشبيه أن العرب كانوا إذا أرادوا الإقدام على عمل من الأعمال وأرادوا أن يعرفوا إن كان ذلك العمل يسوقهم إلى خير أو شرٍ، زجروا الطير وأزعجوه فإن طار يمينا استبشروا وإن طار شمالا تشاءموا.

وكانوا كذلك إذا أرادوا أن يقتسموا شيئا أو يعينوا نصيب أحدهم في عطاء أو قسمة يكتبون أسماء المتقاسمين على سهامٍ ويجعلون لتلك السهام ريشا يخفُّ بها اختراقها للهواء ثم يقذفون بها على الشيء المرجو اقتسامه ومن وقع سهمه على شيء أو جزء صار ذلك حظه، وكانت هيئة السهام التي ألحق بها الريش وهي تخترق الهواء تشبه الطيران.

فمثل القرآن الكريم ما كتبه الله تعالى في الأزل من

would scare up, or the arrows which bore the names of each party and landed upon his share. What this means is that every person will be rewarded for his deeds, which have been assured for him, and no part of his portion will be left out or denied him.

Other meanings of the verse include:

(1) The verse contains another similitude, which is that He says, *to his neck*, depicting how every person's acts are fastened to him, the way that a brand is placed on the neck of a camel so that it is not confused with another camel or misplaced with the wrong owner, or bells are put on the collars of animals so that they are not lost. This is a well-known and recognizable image.

(2) The verse alludes to the timeless knowledge of God Most High and His predestining of all actions, and his making each person's deeds like a bird which flies to him, as though God's decree flies from pre-eternity to the instant in which the deed becomes manifest in the world of time. This ought to inspire God's servant to seek refuge with God Most High, to seek to please Him, to be content with whatever He chooses for him, and to have the best possible relationship with Him.

(3) The verse also contains proof that every person is uniquely chosen for his deeds, because God Most High does not reward anyone for the actions of another, nor does He punish anyone for the sins of another. This is affirmed in the following verse, in which our Lord states, *No soul shall bear the burden of another* [Qur'ān 17:15].

الأعمال لأصحابها في الدنيا بالطير الذي يزعج أو بالسهم الذي يحمل اسم صاحبه ويقع على نصيبه والمعنى أن كلّ إنسان مجازى بعمله محصِّلٌ له لا يتخلف عنه ولا ينقص من نصيبه شيء.

وفي الآية خلا ما سبق معان أخرى منها:

(١) تشتمل الآية على تمثيل آخر وهو قوله تعالى (**في عنقه**) حيث مثل هيئة ملازمة الأعمال لأصحابها بهيئة الوسم الذي يوضع في عنق البعير كي لا يختلط بغيره أو يضله صاحبه أو بهيئة الجلاجل التي تربط في أعناق الحيوانات كي لا تضيع وهي صورة معروفة مشهورة.

(٢) في الآية دليل على سابق علم الله تعالى وتقديره للأعمال حيث جعل فعل العبد كأنه يطير إليه، فكأن حكم الله تعالى يطير من عالم الأزل إلى الوقت الذي يظهر فيه ذلك الفعل في عالم الأمد. وهذا داع للعبد أن يلجأ لله تعالى ويرغب إليه ويرضى باختياره ويحسن فيما بينه وبينه.

(٣) في الآية أيضا دليلٌ على اختصاصِ كلِّ أحدٍ بعمل نفسه وذلك لأن الله تعالى لا يكافئ أحدا بعمل أحد، ولا يعذب أحداً بجرمِ أحد وقد تأكدَ هذا المعنى في الآية التي تليها حيث قال ربنا: "**وَلَا تَزِرُ وَازِرَةٌ وِزْرَ أُخْرَى**". (الإسراء: ١٥)

Parable 22: Mercy to Parents

Sūrat al-Isrā' (17), Verse 24

And lower to them the wing of humility out of mercy, and say, "My Lord, have mercy on them, even as they raised me when I was little."

This verse depicts the humbleness and compassion that are called for when interacting with one's parents, likening it to the meekness of a bird when it fears a stronger bird and lowers its wing in humility. What this means is, "Be as humble and meek with your parents as a bird is when it fears a more powerful bird; and let that arise from your mercy and compassion for them. That will make them feel as though you are still their little child, which is the best way to honor them and show consideration to them."

It is also said that the humble posture suggested by the parable is that of a bird when it is not flying, when it lowers its wings and keeps them folded. The verse then follows this by requiring that this humility arise from a tender evocation of the kindness, goodness, and consideration which your parents have shown you. They were always in a position of dignity and protectiveness, but now they have grown weak, and so you ought to lower yourself to a position of humility before them in order to assuage the disquiet that will have arisen in their souls upon finding themselves in need of you.

Other profundities of the verse include the following:

(1) It shifts from speaking of humility toward them out of mercy

المثلُ الثاني والعشرون: الرحمة بالوالدين
سورةُ الإسراء الآية (٢٤)

﴿ وَاخْفِضْ لَهُمَا جَنَاحَ الذُّلِّ مِنَ الرَّحْمَةِ وَقُلْ رَبِّ ارْحَمْهُمَا كَمَا رَبَّيَانِي صَغِيرًا ﴾

صورت هذه الآيةِ التواضعَ والحنان المطلوبان في معاملة الوالدين بهيئة تَذَلُّلِ الطائر حين يخاف من طائر أشد منه حيث يخفضُ جناحه متذللا. والمعنى على هذا: تواضع لوالديك وتخشع لهما مثلَ تذلل الطائر حال خوفه من طائر أشد منه وأقوى واجعل ذلك ناشئا عن رحمتك وتلطفك بهما حيث إنَّ إشعارهما بأنك لازلت ضعيفاً فيه غايةُ البرِّ ومراعاةُ النَّفسيةِ.

ويُقالُ إنَّ الهيئةَ التي مثل بها التواضع هي هيئة الطائر حال عدم طيرانه حيث يخفض جناحيه ولا ينشُرُهما ثم أعقبت الآية ذلك بطلب أن يكون ذلك ناشئا عن الشفقة لما أسدياه من معروف وإحسان ومراعاة للنفسية حيث كانا على الدوام في محلِّ العزة والمَنَعَةِ وهما اليوم في حال ضعفٍ فصار الأولى بالولد أنْ يتواضع لهما إلى حد يبلغُ الذلَّ كي يزيلَ وحشةَ نفوسهما الناشئة كونهما محتاجين إليه.

وفي الآية معانٍ جليلة منها:

for them, to a reminder of the importance of asking for mercy from God for them, thereby ascending from speaking of God's servant's mercy to speaking of God's own mercy, which is all the more universal, vast, and far-reaching. The command to pray for mercy for them also indicates that prayers for them are likely to be answered.

(2) The verse ends with the words, *even as they raised me when I was little*, which implies that they raised the child with mercy when he was little, and so the prayer for mercy for them is an act of gratitude for that mercy and an acknowledgement of that favor. This is without doubt one of the purposes of dutifulness to parents, which is that it trains the soul to be grateful and appreciative; and that is a way of emulating one of the qualities of God Himself. Just as we are commanded to be grateful to God Most High for the blessings of creation and provision, we are also commanded to be grateful to our parents for being the means of bringing us into the world and for raising us with mercy. "He who does not thank people, does not thank God."

(3) Another goal of the verse is to strengthen family ties, which leads to a cohesive society that produces generations linked by mutual love and kindness. We can see the effects of the absence of dutifulness toward parents in our societies, which have been torn apart by disrespect, everyone being far apart from each other as though each individual were living alone in a state of self-centeredness. This gives rise to psychological ailments and spiritual malaise. Some traces of the old ways remain, however, in more conservative societies where parents are still honored and afforded their rights.

(١) أنَّه انتقل من الحديث عن التذلل لهما رحمةً بهما إلى التنبيه على ضرورة طلب الرحمة من الله لهما فارتقى من الحديث عن رحمة العبد إلى الحديث عن رحمةِ الله وهي أعم وأوسع وأوصل والأمر بطلب الرحمة لهما مؤذن باستجابة الدعاء لهما.

(٢) في ختم الآية بقوله (**كما ربياني صغيرا**) إشارة إلى اقتران تربيتهما بالرحمة حال صغر الولد فكان طلب الرحمة لهما من باب الشكر على تلك الرحمة والاعتراف بذلك الجميل. ولاشك أن هذا مقصد من مقاصد البر بالوالدين، وهو تربية النفوسِ على الشكر وٍ الاعتراف بالجميل تخلقا بأخلاق الباري سبحانه؛ فكما أُمِرنا بشكر الله تعالى على نعمة الخلق والرزق، أُمِرنا بشكر الوالدين على الإيجاد الصوري والتربية والرحمة فمن لم يشكر النّاسَ لم يشكُر الله.

(٣) تهدف الآيةُ بهذا الأمر أيضا إلى تقوية أواصر العائلةِ وهوٍ ما يُنتِجُ مجتمعا متماسكا تخرُجُ الأجيالُ الناشئةُ فيه محبةً مُحسِنَةً مترابطة. ونحنُ نرى أثر غياب البرِّ بالوالدين في مجتَمَعاتِنا التي مزقها العقوق وباعدَ بين أفرادِها فكأنَّ كلَّ فردٍ فيها يعيش وحده في أنانية وأثرةٍ تنتهبهُ الأمراض النفسية والعلل الروحية. ولم تزل بقيةٌ في المجتمعات المحافظة التي لا تزال توقر الوالدين وتعرف حقوقهما.

Parable 23: Between Miserliness and Extravagance

Sūrat al-Isrā' (17), Verse 29

And do not keep your hand chained to your neck, nor open it completely, lest you end up condemned and destitute.

This verse compares miserliness and meanness to chaining one's hand to one's neck, and likens extravagance and wastefulness to opening one's hand completely. The person who is stingy with money is like someone whose hand is chained to his neck so that he cannot utilize it or gain any benefit from it; the wasteful person is like someone who stretches out his hand as far as it will go, exposing himself to pain and aggression.

This parable is based upon visualizing the hand as the source of giving and expending—a recognized convention of the language of the Arabs, who use the word "hand" to symbolize bounty and favor, saying, "So-and-So is a hand to his brethren," and this is understood as indicating that he is bountiful to them. Take for example the words of the poet al-Aʿshā:[27]

Your hands are hands of sincere friendship:
One lends help, the other gives unstintingly.

27: Maymūn ibn Qays al-Aʿshā (d. c. 625 CE) was a Christian pre-Islamic poet from Yamama in Arabia, sometimes numbered among one of the authors of the seven *Muʿallaqāt*.

المثلُ الثالثِ والعشرون: بين الشح والسَّرَف
سورةُ الإسراء الآية (٢٩)

﴿ وَلَا تَجْعَلْ يَدَكَ مَغْلُولَةً إِلَىٰ عُنُقِكَ وَلَا تَبْسُطْهَا كُلَّ الْبَسْطِ فَتَقْعُدَ مَلُومًا مَحْسُورًا ﴾

مثلت هذه الآيةُ الشحَّ والإمساكَ بغَلِّ اليدِ إلى العُنُقِ كما مثَّلت التَّبذيرَ والإسرافَ ببَسْطِ اليدِ غَايَةَ البَسْطِ. وعليهِ فإنَّ الشحيحَ بالمالِ يُشبهُ مَنْ غُلَّتْ يده إلى عُنُقِهِ فلا يستطيع أن يتصرف أو ينتفع بها كما يُشبهُ المسرفُ باسطَ يده غايةِ البسطِ مما يترتبُ عليه الألمَ والتعدي.

وهذا التشبيهُ مبنيٌّ على تَخَيُّلِ اليد مصدراً للبذلِ والعطاءِ وهو أمرٌ معروف في لغةِ العرب حيث يستخدمون لفظة اليد، يرمزون بها للفضل والنعمة فإذا قالوا: "لفلانٍ يدٌ على إخوانه" فُهِمَ من ذلك أن له فضلا عليهم. ومنه قول الأعشى:

يداكَ يدا صدقٍ فكفٌّ مفيدةٌ
وكفٌّ إذا ما ضُنَّ بالمالِ تُنْفِقُ

وقول المتنبي:

And al-Mutanabbī[28] said:

> He has hands which have showered me with gifts;
> I can count some, but cannot enumerate all.

Consider also how God Most High informs us of the shameful false claim which the Jews leveled against Him, Incomparably Glorious is He: *The Jews say, "God's hand is fettered"* [Qur'ān 5:64], by which they meant to accuse Him of stinginess and meanness—though He is far above such a thing. He refuted them by saying, *No, but His Hands are outspread* [Qur'ān 5:64], meaning that He is the All-Generous, Glorious and Majestic is He.

The other many subtleties of the verse include:

(1) It implicitly provides us with instruction regarding a certain value, that of moderation, a trait which is part of true wisdom. This verse explains clearly that the praiseworthy way to give is to find the middle point between the upper and lower extremes. According to the science of ethics, every character trait has two extremes and a middle point. The two extremes are excess and negligence, which are blameworthy due to the harms they cause, whereas the middle point is praiseworthy because it conforms to what is right and just. The two blameworthy extremes here are stinginess, which is harmful for the poor and also for the wealthy, sowing the seeds of discord and hatred between them; and extravagance, which squanders that which family members have a right to and leads to money being spent improperly and unjustifiably. The middle point between the two is what is advocated in this verse, which is moderation in spending, so that one maintains a position between the two prohibitions (*do not ... nor*), avoiding both stinginess and extravagance.

(2) The verse delivers that lofty piece of wisdom, instruction, and

---

28: Aḥmad ibn Ḥusayn, known as al-Mutanabbī (d. 354/965) was a highly celebrated and influential Abbasid-era poet.

له أيادٍ علي سابغة
أعدُّ منها ولا أُعَدِّدُها

ومنه قول الله تعالى حكاية عن ادعاء اليهود وافتراءهم عليه سبحانه: "**وقالت اليهودُ يدُ الله مغلوله**" أي وصفوه بالشح والبخل- تعالى عن ذلك علوا كبيرا- ورده عليهم بقوله: "**بل يداه مبسوطتان**" أي هو الكريم جلَّ شأنه.

وفي الآية لطائف عديدة منها:

(١) أنها اشتملت في محتواها على تعليم حقيقة من الحقائق الدقيقة وهي خلق الاعتدال فكانت من الحكمة. فقد بينت أن المحمود في العطاء هو التوسط بين الإفراط والتفريط. وقد جاء في علم الأخلاق أنَّ لكلِّ خُلُق طرفين ووسطا؛ فالطرفان إفراط وتفريط وهما مذمومان لما يترتب عليهما من المفاسد والوسط محمود لموافقته الحق. والطرفان المذمومان هنا هما الشح الذي يفسد حال المحتاجين وحال صاحب المال ويبذر بذور الكراهية والبغضاء بينهما، والتبذير الذي يضيع حقوق الأقارب ويؤدي لوضع المال في غير محله وصرفه في غير مصرفه. والوسط بين الاثنين ما جاء في الآية وهو الاعتدال في النفقة والوقوف بين النهيين (لا و لا) والعدول عن الحالين الشح والإسراف.

(٢) أنّها صاغت تلك الحكمة الرفيعة وهذا التعليم الراقي والأدب السامق في قالبٍ بلاغي تمثيلي لطيف وهو تصوير الشحيح بمن غلت يده لعنقهِ فتعطلت منفعتها بالكلية

ethical conduct in a subtle and parabolic rhetorical form, likening the stingy person to someone whose hand is chained to his neck, rendering it entirely useless, and depicting the profligate person as someone whose hand is so exaggeratedly open that it will only lead to harm and miss out on all benefit. Presenting lofty concepts in rhetorical form helps to make them understandable, relatable, and practicable, since it has a greater impact upon the soul.

(3) The verse describes the results of the two states, with the consequences of violating the two prohibitions listed respectively, meaning that the consequences are given in the same order as the prohibitions, the first referring to the first, and the second to the second. Hence it says, *lest you should end up condemned*, which is the consequence of stinginess, *and destitute*, which is the consequence of extravagance. Condemnation is the consequence of stinginess because a stingy person is always condemned; indeed, calling him stingy is enough to condemn him. Jāḥiẓ wrote a discourse on the subject in *Akhbār al-bukhalā'*.[29] The poet Abūl-ʿAtāhiyya conp demned misers with these words:

> If you catch one whiff of the miser,
> You'll find it the foulest of bad smells!

The pre-Islamic poet Zuhayr[30] said:

> A man of means who is mean to his people
> With his means should be left to himself
> and condemned.

29: Abū ʿUthmān ʿAmr al-Kinānī, better known as Jāḥiẓ (d. 255/868), was a polymath and author of the Abbasid era from Basra. His *Akhbār al-bukhalā'* was translated as *The Book of Misers* by R.B. Serjeant (Reading, 1995).
30: Zuhayr ibn Abī Sulmā (d. c. 609 CE) was a pre-Islamic Arabian poet, author of one of the seven *Muʿallaqāt*.

وتصوير المسرف بمن بسط يده إلى النهاية فحصل له بذلك الضرر وتجاوز بها كل نفع. وصياغة المعاني الرائقة في القوالب البليغة مما يعين على تفهمها وتقبلها وييسر العمل إذ تكون أعظم أثرا في النفوس.

(٣) أنَّ الآيةَ ذكرت نتيجة الحالين، وجواب النهيين على طريقة النشر المرتب - أي موزعةً بنفس ترتيب النهيين فالأول راجع للأول والثاني راجع للثاني- فقالت: "**فتقعد ملوماً**" واللوم نتيجة الشح ثم قالت "**محسورا**" والحسرة نتيجة الإسراف. أما كون اللوم نتيجة للشح فذلك لأن الشحيح دائما مذموم، بل كفى بوصف الشح ذماً. وقد كتبَ الجاحظ من ذلك طرفا في أخبار البخلاء فطالعه. ومن ذمهم الشحيح قول أبي العتاهية:

إنّكَ إنْ تَسْتَنشِقْ الشحيحا
ألفيته أقبحَ شيء ريحا

وقول زهيرٍ في الجاهلية:

وَمَنْ يكُ ذَا فَضْلٍ فَيَبْخَلْ بِفَضْلِهِ
عَلَى قَوْمِهِ يُسْتَغْنَ عَنْهُ وَ يُذْمَمُ

وأَمَّا كون الحسرة- وهي إنهاك القوى وذهاب القدرة بالكلية- مترتبة على الإسراف فظاهرٌ، حيث إنَّ من يُذهِبُ ريحَهُ

It is obvious why destitution, meaning the total loss of power and resources, is the consequence of extravagance, for when a person squanders his resources and fritters away his money, he will end up powerless and defenseless. That is why moderation is best, and perfection in spending lies in balance. As the saying goes, "The best things are the middle ones, rushing is the worst way to travel, and good lies between two evils." There is also a saying, "Be level headed and moderate; do not aim too low or too high."

ويُتْلِفُ مَالَه يصير بلا قوةٍ ولا مَنَعَةٍ. ولذلك كان التوسط خير حال، وأكمل الإنفاق في الاعتدال. وقد قيلَ: "خيرُ الأمورِ أوساطها وشرُّ السير الحقحقة والحسنةُ بين السيئتين." وقيل أيضا: "عليكَ بالسداد والاقتصادِ ولا وكسَ ولا شططَ."

Parable 24: The Rolled-Up Pages

Sūrat al-Anbiyā' (21), Verse 104

The Day We roll up the heaven as a written scroll is rolled up. As We began the first creation, so shall We repeat it, a promise binding upon Us. Truly, this We shall do.

In this verse, God likens the rolling-up and gathering of the heavens, when its parts will be enfolded upon one another on the Day of Resurrection, to how a scribe rolls up his pages. The word *sijill* (scribe) can mean the page on which something is written, but it can also mean the writer himself. Some say that it means 'page' here and that the verse means, 'as a page of writings is rolled up (by the scribe).'

The purpose of this parable is to depict the event of the Resurrection and to emphasize it by mentioning it again, and affirming God's absolute power which nothing can challenge or delimit. The idolaters rejected the Resurrection and considered it to be impossible that it could occur after the annihilation of the body and the decay of the bones. They used to say, "There is no life but that of this world, and it is simply that wombs produce, and the earth devours." The Qur'ān repeatedly affirms the reality of the Resurrection and stresses how easy such a feat would be for the One Who began creation in the first place. Hence this verse concludes with the words, *As We began the first creation, so shall We repeat it,* emphasizing the point and observing that He Who has the power to create is well able to repeat the act.

المثلُ الرابعِ والعشرون: كـ: طيّ الكُتُب
سورةُ الأنبياء الآية (١٠٤)

﴿ يَوْمَ نَطْوِي السَّمَاءَ كَطَيِّ السِّجِلِّ لِلْكُتُبِ كَمَا بَدَأْنَا أَوَّلَ خَلْقٍ نُعِيدُهُ وَعْدًا عَلَيْنَا إِنَّا كُنَّا فَاعِلِينَ ﴾

مثّلَ الله تعالى في هذه الآية طيَّ السماء وجمعها وردَّ بعض أجزائها على بعضٍ يوم القيامة بطيّ كاتبِ الصحيفةِ لصحيفتهِ. فكلمة 'السجل' تطلقُ على الورقةِ التي يكتب فيها كما تطلقُ على كاتبِ الصحيفة وقيل: الجُملَةُ على تقديرِ مُضافٍ محذوف أي: كَطيِّ صاحبَ السجلِ للكُتُبِ.

والغرضَ من هذا المثل الاستدلال على وقوعِ البعثِ وتأكيدهُ بإعادةِ ذكره والتنبيه على قدرة الله المُطلَقةِ التي لا يعجزها ولا يحدها شيء. وقد كان المشركون ينكرون البعث ويُحيلون وقوعه بعد فناء الأجسامِ وبلى العِظَام ويقولون لا حياةَ سوى هذه الدُّنيا وإنما هي أرحامٌ تدفع وأرض تبلَع، فنبَّه القرآن في غير موضع على وقوع البعث والنشر وأكد على سهولة ذلك على مَنْ أنشأ الخَلْقَ أول مرةٍ ولذلك جاء ختام هذه الآية: "**كَمَا بَدَأْنَا أَوَّلَ خَلْقٍ نُعِيدُهُ**" مؤكدا المعنى ومنبها على أنَّ مَنْ مِن شأنِه الخلق، لا يعجزهُ الإعادة.

The other meanings of this verse include:

(1) Rolling-up heaven means relocating its constituents and bringing them closer together, just as the edges of a flat page are brought together when it is rolled up. This signifies the breakdown of the order of things which prevails today. The Qur'ān speaks about the details of this in several suras. The verse speaks of the collapse of order, not the disappearance of the heavens.

(2) The choice of rolling-up is a subtle hint alluding to the conclusion of deeds and lives, because documents and clothes are usually only folded when they are no longer serviceable or being used. The choice of rolling-up therefore implies the end of that page and the conclusion of that life.

(3) The use of the first-person plural "We" and the singular noun "heaven" is an indication as to how easy and simple that action will be.

ومما يتعلق بالآية من المعاني:

(١) أنَّ طي السماء معناه تغير مواقع أجرامِها واقتراب بعضها من بعض كما تتغير أطراف الورقة المنشورة حين تطوى وذلك دليل على انقراض النظام القائم الآن وقد تكلم القرآن عن تفاصيل ذلك في غير سورة. فالآية تدلُّ على اختلال النظام لا على اضمحلال السماوات.

(٢) في اختيار الطي ملمحٌ لطيفٌ وهو الإشارة إلى انقضاءِ الأعمالِ والأعمارِ إذ إن الصُّحُفَ والألبِسَةَ غالبا ما تُطوى حين لا يبقى لها ثمةَ استخدام أو استعمالٍ فكان اختيار الطي مؤذنٌ بانقضاء تلك الصفحةِ وانتهاء تلك الحياةِ.

(٣) وفي اختيار "نون" المتحدث عن نفسه مع إفراد لفظ السماء إشارة ليسر ذلك الأمر وسهولته.

Parable 25: Worshiping Upon the Brink
Sūrat al-Ḥajj (22), Verse 11

And among mankind is he who worships God upon a brink: if good befalls him, he is content with it; but if an ordeal befalls him, he turns about-face, losing both this world and the Hereafter. That is the manifest loss.

This verse depicts the state of the hypocrite who wavers in his action and is hesitant about his religion, desiring only to reap spoils and gain immediate benefits. It likens him to a person who walks upon the brink of a cliff or a river, at risk of toppling over it; or to someone who stays at the outer edge of the army during a battle, and if he senses the prospect of spoils he holds his ground, feeling at ease, but if he senses defeat or some other setback he turns on his heels and flees.

So the verse describes those who treat faith and obedience speculatively: not rejecting them altogether but not accepting them fully either, but rather weighing them against their previous way of life. Ibn ʿAbbās ﷺ said, "Sometimes a man would come to Medina, and if his wife bore him a son and he made good money, he would be content and say, 'This is a good religion!' But if he fell into poverty and his wife bore him a daughter or had no children, he would say, 'This is a bad religion!' and apostatize."

There are many examples of this in Prophetic biography. Ḍaḥḥāk related that a group of those prospective converts who had been

المثلُ الخامسِ والعشرون: العبادة على حرف سورةُ الحج الآية (١١)

﴿ وَمِنَ النَّاسِ مَنْ يَعْبُدُ اللَّهَ عَلَى حَرْفٍ فَإِنْ أَصَابَهُ خَيْرٌ اطْمَأَنَّ بِهِ وَإِنْ أَصَابَتْهُ فِتْنَةٌ انقَلَبَ عَلَى وَجْهِهِ خَسِرَ الدُّنْيَا وَالْآخِرَةَ ذَلِكَ هُوَ الْخُسْرَانُ الْمُبِينُ ﴾

مثلت هذه الآية حال المنافق المتردد في عمله المضطرب في دينه الساعي وراء الغنيمة وعاجلِ المَنفَعةِ بحال من يمشي على حرف جبلٍ أو وادٍ فهو متهيئ أن يزلَّ عنه. أو بحال من يكون على طرَفِ العَسكرِ في المعركة فإن أحسّ بغنيمة قرَّ واطمأنَّ وإن أحس بهزيمةٍ أو غيرِ ذلك فرَّ ونكص على عقبه.

فالآية تصف إذا أولئك الذين يضعون الإيمان والطاعةَ موضع اختبارٍ، فلا يعرضون عنهما تماما ولا يقبلونهما تماما بل يوازنون بينهما وبين ما كانوا عليه قبلهما. قال ابن عباس رضي الله عنهما: كان الرجلُ يَقدُمُ إلى المدينةِ فإن ولدت امرأتُهُ غلاماً وكثر ماله وماشيته رضي واطمأنَّ وقال هذا دين صالحٌ وإن أصابه وَجَعٌ وولدت امرأته فتاةً أو لم تَلِد قال هذا دينُ سوءٍ فارتدَّ عنه.

given favors to win over their hearts, such as Aqraʿ ibn Ḥābis and ʿAbbās ibn Mirdās, said to one another, "Let us join Muḥammad's religion. If we meet with good, we will know that it is the truth. If we do not, we will know that it is false."

Abū Saʿīd al-Khudrī ﷺ related that a Jewish man converted to Islam and then lost his sight, his wealth, and his son. He said, "Messenger of God, let me resign, for I have not found any good from this religion of mine. My sight, my son, and my wealth are all gone." The Messenger of God ﷺ replied, "Islam is not something you resign from. Islam smelts you, just as fire smelts the dross from iron, gold, and silver."[31]

Other subtleties of this verse include:

(1) The exact nature of the "brink" (*ḥarf*) is left undefined, which has led scholars to take different views regarding it. Ḥasan [al-Baṣrī] said, "The support of religion is the heart and the tongue, and so they are its edges. If each is in harmony with the other, religion is whole. If a man displays religion with his tongue but there is hypocrisy in his heart, one may say that he worships upon a brink." The soundest opinion is that *ḥarf* means the edge of anything, and that the image evoked here is that of someone who walks upon the edge of a river or a cliff.

(2) The verse shows that vacillation (*takhlīṭ*) [or trying to "have the best of both worlds"] is of no benefit to those who suffer from it, even if they may be deceived by its persisting for a while [without apparent harm]. The Companions, may God be well-pleased with them, were people of steadfastness; their goal was God, and their aim was His approval.

31: Suyūṭī, *al-Durr al-manthūr fil-tafsīr bil-manthūr* 6/14.

أمثلةُ هؤلاء كثيرة في السيرة النبوية فقد روى الضحاكُ أنَّ جماعةً من المؤلفةِ قلوبهم كالأقرعِ بن حابِس والعبَّاسِ بن مِردَاس قال بعضُهُم لبعضٍ: ندخُلُ في دين محمدٍ فإن أصبْنَا خيراً عرفنا أنه حقٌّ وإنْ أصبْنا غيرَ ذلكَ عرفنا أنَّه باطِلٌ.

وروى أبو سعيدٍ الخُدُريِّ رضي الله عنه أن رجلا من اليهود أسلم فذهب بصرهُ وماله وولده فقال يا رسول الله أَقِلني فإنِّي لم أُصِبْ من ديني هذا خيرا، ذهب بصري وولدي ومالي. فقال رسول الله ﷺ له: إنَّ الإسلام لا يقال، إنَّ الإسلام ليَسْبِكُ كما تَسْبِكُ النَّارُ خبَثَ الحديدِ والذَّهبِ والفِضَّةِ.

وَ مما يتعلَّقُ بهذهِ الآية من اللطائفِ:

(١) أنها أَبْهَمَت معنى الحرف المقصود، فذهب العلماء فيه مذاهب. قال الحسنُ: إنَّ مُعْتَمَدَ الدين القلب واللسان فهما حرفاه فإن وافق أحدُهُما الآخرَ تكاملَ الدينُ وإذا أظهر بلسانِه الدين وفي قلبه النِّفاقُ قيل: يَعبُدُ على حرفٍ. والمعنى الأقوى هنا في الحرف أنَّهُ الطرفَ من كلِّ شيء فشبه بمن يسير على حرف الوادي أو الجبل أو الوادي.

(٢) قلت: دلّت الآيةُ على أنَّ التخليطَ لا يَنفَعُ أهله وإن انخدعوا ببقاءه حيناً وما كان الصحابة رضوان الله عليهم إلا أهل ثبات مقصودهم الله ومطلوبهم رضاه.

Parable 26: The Light of the Heavens and The Earth

Sūrat al-Nūr (24), Verse 35

God is the Light of the heavens and the earth. The likeness of His Light is as a niche wherein is a lamp. The lamp is in a glass; the glass is as a glittering star, kindled from a blessed tree, an olive neither of the east nor of the west. Its oil would well-nigh shine forth, though no fire touched it. Light upon light! God guides to His Light whom He will; and God devises similitudes for mankind; and God knows all things.

This verse depicts divine guidance and the clear signs which point to it, likening them in their clarity and brilliance to a niche containing a glass of the utmost lucidity, in which there is a lamp fueled with oil which is extremely pure and which, what is more, is blessed oil, balanced in constitution, drawn from an olive tree standing in a place which is level so that the sun reaches it from all sides, allowing it to bask in its warmth. The purpose of this parable is to illustrate the perfect clarity of these divine signs, and how they are as plain, clear, and luminous as can be. The depiction of the lamp as being in a glass suggests that its rays are concentrated and augmented; and likewise, the divine signs are tremendously bright. The lucidity of the lamp's glass increases its light many times over; and the fact that the oil which kindles the lamp is itself pure and refined eliminates the possibility of any blemish appearing to spoil that light. A fourth aspect of this is that the oil is drawn from an olive tree which is

المثلُ السادس والعشرون: نور السماوات والأرض
سورةُ النور الآية (٣٥)

﴿ اللَّهُ نُورُ السَّمَاوَاتِ وَالْأَرْضِ مَثَلُ نُورِهِ كَمِشْكَاةٍ فِيهَا مِصْبَاحٌ الْمِصْبَاحُ فِي زُجَاجَةٍ الزُّجَاجَةُ كَأَنَّهَا كَوْكَبٌ دُرِّيٌّ يُوقَدُ مِنْ شَجَرَةٍ مُبَارَكَةٍ زَيْتُونَةٍ لَا شَرْقِيَّةٍ وَلَا غَرْبِيَّةٍ يَكَادُ زَيْتُهَا يُضِيءُ وَلَوْ لَمْ تَمْسَسْهُ نَارٌ نُورٌ عَلَى نُورٍ يَهْدِي اللَّهُ لِنُورِهِ مَنْ يَشَاءُ وَيَضْرِبُ اللَّهُ الْأَمْثَالَ لِلنَّاسِ وَاللَّهُ بِكُلِّ شَيْءٍ عَلِيمٌ ﴾

مثلت هذه الآية الهداية الربانية والآيات الظاهرات الدالة عليها في جلاءها ووضوحها بمشكاة فيها زجاجة قد بلغت الغاية في الصفاء وفي داخل الزجاجة مصباحٌ يتَّقِدُ بزيتٍ قد بلغَ هو الآخر النهاية في الصفاء، وهو فوق هذا زيت مبارك مُعتدلُ القوام استلَّ من شجرةِ زيتونٍ في محل وسطٍ تنالها الشمس من كل جانب فتتمتع بالدفء. والغرض من ذلك التشبيه بيان كمالِ وضوح هذه الآيات الربانية وأنها قد بلغت الغاية في الشفافية والجلاء والإشراق. فمن جهة كون المصباح في زجاجةٍ يفيد اجتماع اشعته وزيادة نوره وكذلك الآيات الربانية نورها عظيم، ومن جهةِ صفاء زجاجة المصباح، تتضاعف أنواره، ومن جهة كونِ الزيت الذي يوقد

neither of the east nor of the west, implying that the tree is fully mature and that its oil is pure and completely smokeless.

All of those things augment the purity and brilliance of the light, just as the divine signs are clear and brilliant in their material, form, position, address, and source, never besmirched by the least suggestion of doubt or marred by the slightest suspicion of inadequacy. They are all pure blessing, ease, and light.

It has been said that the meaning of the verse is to liken the Prophet ﷺ to a niche which contains a glass inside which is a lamp fueled by pure, luminous, blessed oil. In that interpretation, the niche would be his ﷺ body, the glass his breast, the lamp his heart, the oil his innermost secret and spirit, and the tree would be Abraham ﷺ, the source of his Prophethood. Several of the Followers preferred that opinion, including ʿAṭā᾿ ibn Abī Rabāḥ. It also accords with the fact that God Most High calls him *an illuminating lamp* [Qur᾿ān 33:46].

The many subtleties of this verse include:

(1) The word "lamp" is repeated because it is the most crucial element of the parable, and the word "glass" is repeated for the same reason. The rhetoricians call this sort of repetition *tashābuh al-aṭrāf* ("end-matching"; anadiplosis). An example of it is found in the words of the poet Laylā al-Akhyaliyya:[32]

> When Ḥajjāj alights in an ailing land,
> He tracks down its most extreme ill and he cures it,
> Cures it of the chronic ailment that has stricken it;
> When a young man brandishes his lance, he bloods it!

(2) It occurs to my heart that *neither of the east nor of the west* contains an allusion to the land of Arabia, which is south of Syria, Iraq, and Egypt and is not described as east or west, and which contains Mecca, the Mother of Towns. It is as though the Prophet ﷺ were the

32: Laylā al-Akhyaliyya (d. c. 90/709) was an Arab poet of the Umayyad era.

به المصباح منيرا بذاته صافيا رقيقا، ينفي حدوث او طروّ أي كدر على ذلك النور. ومن جهة رابعةٍ، فإن استلال ذلك الزيت من شجرة زيتون لا شرقية ولا غربية، يفيد تمام نُضج تلك الشجرة وصفاء زيتها وعدم ترتب الدخان عليه. وكلُّ هذه الأمور تزيد في صفاء الضوء وسطوعه، وكذلك الآيات الربانية فهي من حيث مادتها وصورتها وموقعها وخطابها ومصدرها جلية بهية لا تعتريها شائبةُ وَهم، ولا تَعتَورِها عائبةُ قصور، بل كُلُّها بركة ويسر ونور.

وقيل، بل المراد في الآية تشبيه النبي ﷺ بالمشكاة التي تشتمل على زجاجة بها مصباح يتقد بزيت خالص منير مبارك. وعلى هذا فتكون المشكاة جسمه، والزجاجة صدره، والمصباح قلبه والزيت سره وروحه ﷺ والشجرة إبراهيم عليه السلام معدن نبوته. وقد اختار هذا القول عدد من التابعين منهم عطاء بن أبي رباح وهو يتسق مع قول الله تعالى في حقه ﷺ: **"وسراجاً منيرا"**

ومِن لطائف هذه الآية- ولطائفها كثيرةٌ:

(١) إعادةُ لفظةِ (المصباحِ) لأنه أعظم أركان التمثيل وكذلك إعادةُ لفظة (الزجاجة) للسبب نفسه. وهذه الإعادة تسمى عند البلاغيين "تشابُهُ الأطراف" ومنها قول ليلى الأخيلية:

إذا أُنـزِلَ الحجاجُ أرضـا مريضةً
تتبع أقصى دائها فشفاهـا
شفاها من الداء العضال الذي بها
غلامٌ إذا هزَّ القناة سقاها

lamp, Mecca the glass, and the lands of the Arabs the niche, which is illuminated by his light and from which the light is disseminated across the world. The oil is his Prophethood, drawn from the tree of Abraham the Close Friend of God عليه السلام. There is a great deal that could be said about this parable; it is one of those subjects that no expert could do full justice to.

(٢) وقع في القلبِ أنَّ قوله "**لاشرقية ولا غربية**" فيه إشارة لبلاد العرب فهي في جنوب الشام والعراق ومصر، لا توصف بشرق ولا غرب، وفيها مكة أم القرى فكأنه صلوات الله وسلامه عليه هو المصباح ومكة هي الزجاجة وبلاد العرب المشكاة التي تضيء بنوره ومنها يشع النور في جنبات الأرض. والزيت نبوته المستمدة من شجرة إبراهيم الخليل عليه السلام. والكلام في هذا المثال يطول وهو مما يعي الفحول.

Chapter 27: A Mirage in the Desert
Sūrat al-Nūr (24), Verse 39

As for those who disbelieve, their works are like a mirage in the desert which the thirsty man takes to be water, until he comes to it and finds it to be nothing; but he finds God there, and He pays him his account in full; and God is swift in reckoning.

This verse depicts the state of an unbeliever who strives to do virtuous deeds, supposing that they will benefit him, and who frequently engages in them, though they will not be of any avail to him on the Day of Resurrection, when instead he will be severely punished. It likens him to a thirsty man who sees a mirage and takes it to be water, so his heart becomes attached to it and he rushes toward it as fast as he can. However, when he gets to the spot where he imagined the water to be, he finds no water, but only an antagonist who captures and punishes him, subjecting him to serious harm. He feels immense woe and disappointment upon not gaining what he thought he would, but suffering instead something that had never crossed his mind.

A mirage (*sarāb*) is an optical illusion which occurs in waterless deserts at midmorning time, which looks like running water but is not water. According to al-Aṣmaʿī[33] the words *sarāb* and *āl* mean the

33: ʿAbd al-Malik al-Aṣmaʿī (d. 213/828) was a renowned grammarian and polp ymath of Basra.

المثلُ السابع والعشرون: كـ: سرابٍ بقيعة سورةُ النور الآية (٣٩)

﴿ وَالَّذِينَ كَفَرُوا أَعْمَالُهُمْ كَسَرَابٍ بِقِيعَةٍ يَحْسَبُهُ الظَّمْآنُ مَاءً حَتَّى إِذَا جَاءَهُ لَمْ يَجِدْهُ شَيْئًا وَوَجَدَ اللَّهَ عِنْدَهُ فَوَفَّاهُ حِسَابَهُ وَاللَّهُ سَرِيعُ الْحِسَابِ ﴾

مثلت هذه الآية حال الكافرِ في الكدِّ في أعمالِ البرِّ ظنًّا أنها تنفعُهُ والدخولِ فيها مستكثرا منها مع كونها لا تنفعه يوم القيامة بل يقع له العقاب العظيم بحالِ ظمآنٍ يرى السرابَ فيحسبه ماءً فيتعلق قلبه به ويسعى إليه السعى الحثيث فإذا بلغَ تلك البقعةَ التي خال أنها موقعَ الماء لم يجد ماءً ووجد عنده غريماً يأسره ويعاقبه وينزل به الضرر الشديد فعَظُمَ همّه واشتدت حسرته لعدم حصول ما كانَ يظُن ووقوع ما لم يخطر على باله.

والسراب هو ما يتراءى للعين وقت الضحى الأكبر في الفلوات شبيه الماء الجاري وليس بماء وقال الأصمعي: السراب والآل شيءٌ واحدٌ. وقال بعضهم: بل هما شيئان فالسراب يكون بعد الزوال والآل من الضحى إلى زوال الشمس. قال يونس: الآل مُذْ غدوة إلى ارتفاع الضحى

same thing; but others say that they are different: the *sarāb* occurs after midday, while the *āl* occurs from midmorning to noon. Yūnus[34] says that *āl* means a mirage occurring between morning and high midmorning, and then the term *sarāb* is used for one occurring during the rest of the day. Ibn al-Sikkīt[35] says that *āl* means an illusion of rising figures which is seen at midmorning, and *sarāb* means an illusion of water flowing on the ground which is seen at midday.

The nature of the resemblance between the two scenarios is that even if the unbeliever was someone who performed virtuous deeds, he deserves no reward for them; but if he was someone who committed sinful deeds, he deserves punishment for them, even though he may believe otherwise. So when he comes to the Resurrection only to find not reward but a terrible punishment, he will be appallingly remorseful and woe-stricken. His state will resemble that of a thirsty man in dire need of water who sees a mirage and becomes heartened by it, hoping for salvation and filled with anticipation; but when he gets there and finds his hopes dashed, his despair will be immense.

Other subtleties of the verse include:

(1) The parable is composed of several parts, and can be broken down as follows: [i] The deeds are like a mirage; [ii] the unbeliever is like a thirsty man in the way he needs to benefit from his deeds; [iii] he will be disappointed at the Reckoning just as the thirsty man is disappointed; [iv] the unbeliever's surprise at the Reckoning will resemble that of a man who finds someone lying in wait to capture him.

(2) In this parable God Most High compares the state of the unbeliever to that of the believer in the Hereafter. The state of the believer was described in the previous verse by His Words, *That God may reward them for the best of what they did, and give them more out of His bounty* [Qur'ān 24:38], which is a most emphatic way of

34: Yūnus ibn Ḥabīb (d. after 183/798) was a grammarian of Basra.
35: Ya'qūb ibn al-Sikkīt (d. 244/858) was an Abbasid grammarian and poet.

الأعلى ثم هو سرابٌ سائر اليوم. وقال ابن السِّكِّيت: الآل الذي يرفع الشخوص وهو يكون بالضحى والسراب الذي يجري على وجه الأرض كأنه الماء وهو نصفُ النهار.

ووجهُ التشبيه بين الصورتين أنَّ الذي يأتي به الكافر إن كان من أعمال البرِّ فهو لا يستحق عليها ثوابا وإن كان من أفعال الإثم فهو يستحق عليها عقابا مع اعتقاده خلاف ذلك، فإذا وافى عرصات القيامة ولم يجد ثوابا بل وجد عقابا عظيما اشتدت حسرته وتناهى غمه فأشبه حال ذلك الظمآن الذي اشتدت حاجته للماء فلما شاهد السراب تعلق قلبه به ورجا النجاة وقوي طمعه فلما وصل إليه وأيس مما كان يرجوه عظم غمه.

وفي الآية لطائف منها:

(١) أنَّ التمثيل مركبٌ من أجزاء تصلح للتفريق [١] فالأعمال كالسراب [٢] والكافر كالظمآن في حاجته للانتفاع بعمله [٣] وخيبته عند الحساب كخيبة الظمآن [٤] ومفاجأة الكافر عند الحساب تشبه مفاجأة من وجد من يترصد له لأخذه وأسره.

(٢) أن هذا التمثيل يقابلُ فيه الحق سبحانه وتعالى حال الكافر بحال المؤمن في الآخرة وقد سبق بيان حال المؤمن في الآية السابقة في قوله تعالى: "**لِيَجْزِيَهُمُ اللَّهُ أَحْسَنَ مَا عَمِلُوا وَيَزِيدَهُمْ مِنْ فَضْلِهِ**" وفي هذا أبلغُ الأثرِ وغايةُ التَّفصيلِ وفي المثل التالي سيقابلُ حال الكافرِ في الدنيا بحال المؤمنِ ليمايز بين الفريقين ويباين بين الجانبين وبضدها تتميز الأشياءُ.

expressing the meaning. Then in the next parable, He will contrast the state of the unbeliever in the world with that of the believer, showing the difference between the two factions and contrasting the opposing sides, since that is the best way to differentiate things.

(3) He says of the mirage that he *finds it to be nothing*. Now a mirage is a thing, if only in the mind of the one who beholds it, but what this means is that in reality it is nothing at all because it is devoid of benefit. This is akin to how one says of a person who had no success, "He didn't do anything." Reflect on this.

(4) Books on Arabic linguistics provide us with a subtle point regarding the difference between hope (*rajā'*), anticipation (*ṭam'*), and wish (*amal*). The word *amal* is usually used for things that are unlikely to happen, while *ṭam'* is used for more likely things, and *rajā'* is in between them. The hopeful person might fear that his hope will not be fulfilled, which is why hope is often paired with fear. If the fear is very strong, then *amal* is used because the hoped-for thing is less likely.[36]

36: From the author's private notes.

(٣) أنه قال عن السراب: "**لم يجدهُ شيئا**" والسراب شيءٌ وإن كان في عقل صاحبه فأفاد أنه على التحقيق ليس بشيء لخلوه عن النفع كما يقال فيمن لم ينل حظا: لم يعمل شيئا، فتأمل.

(٤) فائدة لطيفة في الفرق بين الرجاء والطمع والأمل مُستلّةٌ من كُتُبِ اللغة: أكثر ما يُستَعمَلُ الأملُ فيما يستبعدُ حصوله والطمع فيما يقرب حصوله والرجاء بينهما. والراجي قد يخاف ألا يحصلَ مأمُولهُ ولذا يستخدمُ بمعنى الخوف فإذا قوي الخوف استعمل الأمل (**لبُعْدِ المرجو حينئذٍ**). ا.هـ منقولا من كِنّاشتي الخاصة.

Parable 28: The Waves of Darkness

Sūrat al-Nūr (24), Verse 40

Or like the darknesses of a deep sea, covered by waves, above which are waves, above which are clouds, layer upon layer of darknesses! When he holds out his hand, he can scarcely see it. And he to whom God grants no light, has no light.

This verse depicts the unbelievers, likening their beliefs to darknesses which shroud a sailor traveling upon a sea wracked by violent waves which crash over him one after the other due to the violence of the wind. He can barely see a thing because of the intensity of the darkness, finding himself in the midst of the deep sea where the waters stretch far below. In the sea, which is *lujjī*, meaning "deep" like the ocean, the bottom is very dark. When the waves crash over him, the darkness is intense; and when there are clouds above the waves too, the darkness is even more extreme, and the sailor can barely see his own hand, though it is the closest thing to him. So God takes the beliefs of those unbelievers, which surround them and darken their minds and hearts, and likens them to those compound darknesses of the waves, the deep sea, and the clouds. The purpose of the parable is to stress the ignorance of the unbelievers and their inability to see things, so long as they are shrouded by their falsehoods and spurious doctrines.

Other subtleties of the verse include:

المثلُ الثامن والعشرون: لُجَجُ الظُّلُمات
سورةُ النور الآية (٤٠)

﴿ أَوْ كَظُلُمَاتٍ فِي بَحْرٍ لُّجِّيٍّ يَغْشَاهُ مَوْجٌ مِّن فَوْقِهِ مَوْجٌ مِّن فَوْقِهِ سَحَابٌ ظُلُمَاتٌ بَعْضُهَا فَوْقَ بَعْضٍ إِذَا أَخْرَجَ يَدَهُ لَمْ يَكَدْ يَرَاهَا وَمَن لَّمْ يَجْعَلِ اللَّهُ لَهُ نُورًا فَمَا لَهُ مِن نُّورٍ ﴾

صورت هذه الآية الكفارَ في عقائدهم بالظلماتِ التي تغشى راكبَ بحر شديد الموج تركبه الموجات واحدة بعد الأُخرى لشدة الريح فلا يكاد يرى شيئا من شدة الظلمة ووجوده في لجة البحر أي ماؤه الشديد القاع ووسطه البعيد القعر. فالبحر اللجيُّ- أي ذو اللجةِ كالمحيط- يكون قعره مظلما جدا فإذا ترادفت عليه الأمواج اشتدت ظلمته، فإذا كان فوق الأمواج سحابٌ بلغت الظلمةُ غايتها حتى إن الراكب فيه لا يكاد يرى يده وهي أقربُ شيءٍ إليه. فجعل الله تعالى عقائد هؤلاء الكفار وهي تحيطُ بهم وتُظلِمُ عقولَهم وقلوبهم مثل هذه الظلمات المتراكمة من الأمواج والبحر اللجي والسحاب. والمقصود من التمثيل المبالغةُ في جهالة الكفار وعدم قدرتهم على رؤية شيء طالما هم مغمورون في باطلهم وزيفهم. ومن لطائف هذه الآية:

(1) It describes the wave as "covering" the deep sea, which is an allusion to how various kinds of ignorance are self-reinforced and renewed. It does not speak of the existence of the waves, but of their renewal, and then adds to this by implying that there are multiple renewing waves, meaning multiple kinds of ignorance, from the ignorance of fanaticism and appetite to the ignorance of hatred, pride, and so on.

(2) The verse lists three darknesses: that of the deep sea, that of the waves, and that of the gathered clouds. These correspond to the darknesses of the heart, the sight, and the hearing. To explain: when a person is in the depths of the sea, he is surrounded by constant darkness simply by being in the midst of the sea, unable to see anything else around him. This resembles the way that darkness afflicts the heart by shrouding it. Then when waves crash over him, they deafen him to every sound except for themselves, as though they are a darkness and a veil over the hearing. Then when clouds shroud him too, veiling his sight from even the things closest to him, they are like the darkness of sight which prevents the beholding of anything, even what is close at hand. Perhaps there is also an allusion here to darkness of heart, character, and mind. Darkness of heart is like the deep sea because the heart is the center and the axis of the human being. Character displays what the heart contains, and so the waves of character traits are dark, every bad trait that appears being followed by another which is even worse. Then darkness of mind is like a cloud which envelops the person from above, which signifies the ignorance that dominates the mind of the unbeliever.

It has also been said that the three darknesses signify the three states of the unbeliever. First, he does not know, which is like the darkness of the deep sea. Secondly, he does not know that he does not know, which is like the ever-renewing waves, since his ignorance of his own ignorance is always renewing in every instance. Thirdly, he believes that he *does* know, which is like the darkness of a cloud which blinds his sight.

(١) أنها وصفت الموج بأنه (يغشى) البحرَ اللجيّ وذلك إشارةٌ لتجدد أنواع الجهالات، فلم تقل بوجود الموج بل بتجدده ثم زادت ذلك بالإشارة إلى أنها أنواع متجددة من الموج أي أنواع متعددة من الجهالات، فمن جهالة العصبية والشهوات إلى جهالة الكراهية والكبر وغير ذلك.

(٢) أنها عددت ظلماتٍ ثلاث، ظلمةُ البحر اللجي وظلمة الأمواج وظلمة السحاب المتراكم ويقابلها ظلمة القلب وظلمة البصر وظلمة السمع وبيان ذلك أن الإنسان إذا كان في لجة البحر استوليت عليه ظلمة ثابته بكونه وسط الماء لا يرى حوله بعيدا سواه فأشبهت هذه حصول الظلمة في القلب باكتنافها إياه فإذا علت الأمواج حجبت عنه كل صوت سواها فكأنها ظلمة في السمع وحجاب ثم إذا اكتنفه السحاب فحجب رؤيته لأقرب شيء إليه كان كظلمة البصر المانعة من رؤية كل شيء حتى القريب. ولعل الإشارة أيضا إلى ظلمة القلب وظلمةِ الخُلُق وظلمة العقل فظلمة القلب يمثلها البحر اللجي لأن القلب مركز الإنسان وعليه المعول والخلق مظهر ما في القلب فكانت أمواج الأخلاق مظلمة لا يبرز سوء أحدها حتى يلحقه آخرُ أشدَّ منه ثم ظلمة العقل التي تشبه السحاب الذي يحيط بالإنسان مِنْ علٍ والمقصود منها الجهالة التي تستولي على عقل الكافر. وقيل إن الظلمات الثلاث تشبه حالات ثلاث للكافر: فأولها أنه لا يدري وذلك كظلمة لجة البحر والثانية أنه لا يدري أنه لا يدري وذلك كالأمواج المتجددة فعدم علمه بأنه لا يدري متجدد بتجدد المواقف والثالثة أنه يعتقد أنه يدري وذلك يشبه ظلمة السحاب الذي يعمي بصر الإنسان.

Parable 29: Too Late for Regret

Sūrat al-Furqān (25), Verse 27

That Day the wrongdoer will gnaw at his hands, saying, "Oh, if only I had taken a path with the Messenger!"

This verse contains two parables or depictions. The first depicts the state of regret in which the wrongdoer will find himself on the Day of Resurrection, and how he will be overcome with sorrow and pain, likening him to someone who gnaws at his own hands. Gnawing on the hands was a symbol of regret for the Arabs, as they were already familiar with the link between this image, or action, and remorse; so, the verse featured a usage that was familiar to them. Similarly, they would say of an enraged person that he was "biting his fingertips", and hence the Qur'ān uses that imagery in the verse, *They bite their fingertips at you in rage* [Qur'ān 3:119]. All of these are metonyms.

The second parable depicts the concept of emulating and following the Messenger, likening it to following a guide who shows you the right way to get to a particular destination.

This second parable comprises several parts, which can be separated. We might say that the Messenger is represented by the guide, the call by the path. We might also say that the result of following that path, namely arriving at the goal, represents the result of answering the call, which is salvation in the Hereafter and success and happiness in the world.

Other points relating to this verse include the following:

المثلُ التاسعُ والعشرون: فات وقت الندم
سورةُ الفرقان الآية (٢٧)

﴿ وَيَوْمَ يَعَضُّ الظَّالِمُ عَلَى يَدَيْهِ يَقُولُ يَا لَيْتَنِي اتَّخَذْتُ مَعَ الرَّسُولِ سَبِيلًا ﴾

تشتملُ هذه الآيةُ على تمثيلين أو صورتين. أما الصورةُ الأولى فهي تمثيل حال الندم الذي يقع فيه الظالم يوم القيامة وما يعتريه من حسرة وألم بحل مَنْ يَعَضُّ على يديه. والعضُّ على اليدين كناية عن الندمِ عند العربِ حيثُ تعارفوا على ربط هذه الصورةِ أو هذا الفعل بالندم فجاءت الآية القرآنية مشتملةً على ما تعارفوا عليه مثل قولهم في المُغتاظ "يعض على أنامله" وبها جاءَ القرآن في قوله تعالى: "**عضوا عليكم الأنامل من الغيظ**" وكُلُّها كنايات.

والصورة الثانية هي تمثيل لهيئة الإقتداء بالرسول ومتابعته بهيئة مسايرة الدليلِ الذي يُعرِّفُ الإنسانَ بالسيرِ في سبيل معينٍ وقد تضمن هذا التشبيه الأخير عدة أجزاء يمكنُ تفريقها فنشبهُ الرسول بالدليل والدعوة بالسبيل كما يمكن أن نُشبّهَ ما يحصل عن سلوكِ ذلك السبيل من وصول للغاية بما يحصل عن متابعةِ الدعوةِ من نجاةٍ في الآخرة وفلاح وسعادة في الدنيا.

(1) It alludes to an event which occurred in the lifetime of the Messenger ﷺ, which was that there was a man named ʿUqba ibn Abī Muʿīṭ, who was one of the fiercest enemies of the Prophet ﷺ and was also a neighbor of his. It was a custom of his that when he returned from journeys, he would hold a meal for the nobles of his people. One day he invited the Prophet ﷺ to such a meal, and he accepted the invitation, hoping that it might lead to his heart softening somewhat towards his message. When he served him the food, the Prophet ﷺ said, "I cannot eat your food until you testify that there is no god but God." ʿUqba testified—or affected and so the Prophet ﷺ ate. Umayya ibn Khalaf, who was a friend of ʿUqba, was absent at the time. When he returned and was told of what had happened, he said to ʿUqba, "Have you converted, ʿUqba?" He replied, "By God, I have not. All that happened was that a man came to me and refused to eat my food unless I testified for him, and I was ashamed at the prospect of his leaving my house without eating, so I testified for him, and he ate." Umayya said, "I will never be content with you until you go to him and spit in his face!" So ʿUqba declared his unbelief, and did what his close friend had demanded of him.

(2) I believe that this verse elucidates the effect of friendship, and how every person shares the religion of his close friend, whether that spells salvation or ruin for him. Imam ʿAlī ibn Abī Ṭālib, may God ennoble his countenance, said in a poem of his:

> Do not befriend an ignorant man;
> Beware of him, and again beware!
> How many a fool has been the ruin
> Of a sensible man who befriended him!
> Whenever two men walk together,
> Either one will be compared to the other.
> Whenever a heart encounters a heart,
> It will find evidence to learn about it.
> And any two things when juxtaposed
> Invite analogy and comparison.

ومما يتصلُ بهذه الآية:

(١) أنها عقبت على موقف حصل في حياة الرسول ﷺ وذلك أنّ عُقبةَ بن أبي مُعيط كان من أشدّ أعداء النبي ﷺ وكان جاراً له، وكانت عادته (أي عقبة) إذا عاد من سفر أن يصنع طعاما ويدعو له أشراف القوم فدعا النبي ﷺ يوما إلى طعام فأجاب آملا أن يترتب على دعوته شيءٌ من الخير من ترقيق قلبه. فلما قدّم الطعام قال له النبي ﷺ: "ما أنا بآكل طعامك حتى تشهد أن لا إله إلا الله" فشهد - تصنعا- فأكلَ النبي ﷺ. وكانَ أُميةُ بن خلفٍ - وهو صاحب عقبة- غائبا. فلما عاد و أُخبِرَ بذلك قال لعقبةَ: صبأتَ يا عقبة، فقال: والله ما صبأت ولكن دخل عليّ رجلُ فأبى أن يأكل طعامي حتى أشهد له فاستحييت أن يخرج من بيتي ولم يَطعَم فشهدت له فطَعِمَ. فقال أمية: ما أنا بالذي أرضى عنكَ أبداً إلا أن تأتيه فتبصق في وجهه، فكفر عقبةُ وامتثل لما أمره به صاحبه وخليله.

(٢) قلتُ: وقد بينت الآيةُ أثرَ الصاحبِ وأنَّ المرءَ على دينِ خليلهِ، فإما مَنجاةٌ أو مَردَاةٌ. وقد قال الإمام على بن أبي طالب -كرم الله وجهه- في ذلك شعرا:

فلا تـصحب أخا الجهل، وإيــاك وإيــاه
فكم من جاهلٍ أردى، حليما حين آخاه
يقاس المرءُ بالمرءِ، إذا ما هو مــاشــاه
وللقلب على القلب ، دليل حين يلقاه
وللشيء من الشيء ، مقاييسُ وأشباه

Parable 30: A Spiders House
Sūrat al-ʿAnkabūt (29), Verse 41

The parable of those who choose protectors besides God is as the likeness of the spider that makes a house. Truly the frailest of homes is the spider's home, if they only knew.

In this verse, God depicts the state of the idolaters and how they adopt idols which they believe will defend and protect them, though in fact they are too weak to defend even themselves. He likens them to the spider that makes a house for itself of its own weaving, believing that it will protect it from aggressors; but it cannot withstand the slightest pressure, and will fall to pieces.

The spider is appropriate here for several reasons. A house must have a wall to defend, a roof to shelter, a door to close and other useful things. At the very least, it must have a wall to keep out the cold and a roof to protect from the heat. If it does not have those things, then it is not a house at all, but merely a patch of exposed ground. The spider's house does not provide it with shelter or protection. The same is true of those false gods, for the least which can be expected of a deity is that it wards off harm and provides benefit; but they cannot do that, and so adopting them does not achieve anything that would be expected of their like, just as the spider does not satisfy any of the requirements of a house when it weaves its web.

From another perspective, the lowest standard required of a house is that even if it cannot be a cause of stability, peace, and

المثلُ الثلاثون: بيتُ العَنكَبُوتِ
سورةُ العنكبوت الآية (٤١)

﴿ مَثَلُ الَّذِينَ اتَّخَذُوا مِنْ دُونِ اللَّهِ أَوْلِيَاءَ كَمَثَلِ الْعَنْكَبُوتِ اتَّخَذَتْ بَيْتًا وَإِنَّ أَوْهَنَ الْبُيُوتِ لَبَيْتُ الْعَنْكَبُوتِ لَوْ كَانُوا يَعْلَمُونَ ﴾

مثّل الله في هذه الآية حال المشركين في اتخاذهم الأوثان يحسبونها تدفع عنهم وتحميهم بينما هي أضعف من أن تدفع عن أنفسها بحال العنكبوت تتخذ لنفسها من نسجها بيتا تحسب أنها تعتصم به من المعتدي فإذا هو لا يصمد أمام أضعف تحريك فيسقط ويتمزق.

أما وجوه اختيار العنكبوت فذلك لأن البيت ينبغي أن يتوفر له حائط حائل وسقف يظل وباب يغلق وأمور يُنتفعُ بها أو على الأقل حائط يقي البرد وسقف يحفظ من القيظ، فإن لم يحصل شيء من ذلك كان كالبيداء ليس ببيت. وبيت العنكبوت لا يُكِنُّها ولا يُجِنُّها. وكذلك المعبودات الباطلة، فأقل ما يطلب من المعبود دفع الضر وجرُّ النفع وهي لا تقدر على هذا فلم يحصل باتخاذها شيء مما يطلب من مثلها كما لا يحصل للعنكبوت شيء من معاني البيت باتخاذه نسجه بيتا.

ومِن وجهٍ آخر، فإن أدنى مراتب البيت أنه إن لم

tranquility, it should at the very least not be a cause of instability, disturbance, and dissolution. But the spider's house becomes a cause of inconvenience for it, because the resident of the house in which the spider nests will pursue each web it weaves, cleaning them off and removing them from every corner of the house, sweeping them away with a rough and damaging brush. The same is true of the unbeliever, for by worshiping those idols and expending effort to uphold their rights, the least they will do is become a cause of ruin and loss for him. Not only will they not bring him any benefit; they will also cause him great harm, torment, disgrace, and perdition.

These are a few of the many subtleties of the verse:

(1) The spider's house is weak and vile on both the sensory and moral planes. On the sensory plane, that is because it weaves it with the foulest part of itself: its strands are exuded from its rear end, unlike the silkworm's silk, which issues from its mouth. A poet said, "Like the neck of a spider from whose backside a thread was spun." On the moral plane, it is because, the experts say, the female spins the web, but the male destroys it. Also, the female spins the web in preparation for mating, and then after insemination she preys upon the male because its silks are important for the development of the eggs. There are species of spider in which the young feed upon the father and kill the mother before falling upon and slaying one another, in a phenomenon known as spider cannibalism. This illustrates how the spider's house is a place of depravity, on both the sensory and the moral planes.

(2) The Qur᾽ān does not liken the state of such people to the web itself, but rather to the use of the web as a house. That is because the web is not lacking in benefit for the spider since it facilitates the catching of flies, which is a lowly benefit. Likewise, those people do not lose out on the trappings of the world, which are tawdrier in condition and value than flies, but they do lose out on eternal bliss and happiness in the Hereafter. But taking a web as a house is

يكن سببَ ثبات ورفق وطمأنينة ألا يكون سبب شتات وقلق وافتراق لكنَّ بيت العنكبوت يصير سبب إزعاج له، فصاحب البيت - الذي يعشش فيه العنكبوت- يتبعه في كل نسجٍ بالتنظيف والإزالة عن كل زاوية من زوايا البيت والمسح بالمسوح الخشنة المؤذية. وكذلك الكافر فإنه بعبادته لتلك المعبودات وبذل الجهد في إقامة حقوقها لا أقلَّ من ألا تصير سبب بوارٍ وخسارٍ له - إن لم تكن سبب نفع- لكنها تصير مجلبة مضرة وعذاب ومعرةٍ وتباب.

وفي الآية لطائف كثيرة منها:

(١) أن بيت العنكبوت ضعيف قبيح حساً ومعنىً أما حسا فلأنه ينسجه بأخبث ما عنده إذ تخرج خيوطه من دبره بينما ينسج دود القز حريره من فيه. قال الشاعر: قفا عنكبوتٍ سُلَّ من دبرها غزل. وأما في المعنى فذلك لأنه - كما يقول أهل التخصص- بيت ضعيف حيث تنسج الأنثى بينما ينقض الذكر الغزل. كما أنَّ الأنثى تنسج البيت عند الاستعداد للتزاوج وبعد التلقيح تفترس الذكر لأن أنسجته مهمة لإنضاج البيض. وبعض أنواع العنكبوت يأكل الأبناء أباهم ويقتلوا أمهم قبل أن ينقض بعضهم على بعض فيقتل أحدهم الآخر في ظاهرة تعرف بـ ولذلك فهو بيت محروم حساً ومعنى.

(٢) لم يمثل القرآن حالهم "**بالنسج**" وإنما مثله باتخاذ ذلك النسج بيتا وذلك لأن النسج نفسه لا يخلو من فائدة للعنكبوت وهو اصطياده الذباب - وهي فائدة حقيرة- وكذلك

something futile. Likewise, if they were to take those idols, in their powerlessness, as proof for the existence, perfection, and majesty of God, then that would be a source of benefit for them; but to treat them as deities is absurd and foolish in the extreme.

هؤلاء لا يفوتهم من الدنيا متاعها الذي هو أخس حالا وقيمة من الذباب لكن يفوتهم نعيم الأبد وسعادة الآخرة. لكن اتخاذ النسج بيتا أمر باطل وكذلك هذه الأوثان لو اتخذوها -في عجزها- دليلا على وجود الله وكماله وجلاله لكان في ذلك فائدة لهم لكن اتخاذهم لها معبوداتٍ أمر غاية في البطلان والسفه.

Parable 31: The Slave Partners

Sūrat al-Rūm (30), Verse 28

He sets forth for you a parable from yourselves: among those whom your right hands possess, do you have any partners in what We have provided for you, such that you are equal therein, fearing them as you fear your own? Thus do We detail the signs for rational people.

This verse presents us with a parable whose purpose is to refute idolatry and to affirm the Oneness of God and His sole claim to creation and provision. It depicts the self-contradictory position wherein the idolaters claim that their idols are partners to God in power, and that they can protect their worshipers from what God wills for them, be it punishment or something else, while at the same time those idolaters acknowledge that those idols were created by God Most High.

The verse likens that state of affairs to that of people who possess slaves who have become partners in the provisions of their masters, and their equals in word and authority, such that their masters are wary of them when they wish to dispose of those provisions, anxious that they might fail to please their slaves. This latter scenario was inconceivable to the people whom the verse addressed, since it was unimaginable that a slave could question his master's authority or be his equal. So that comparison showed them the error of their ways in considering their idols equal to God Most High despite admitting that they were His creations.

المثلُ الحادي والثلاثين: العبيدُ الشُّركاء
سورةُ الروم الآية (٢٨)

﴿ ضَرَبَ لَكُمْ مَثَلًا مِنْ أَنْفُسِكُمْ هَلْ لَكُمْ مِنْ مَا مَلَكَتْ أَيْمَانُكُمْ مِنْ شُرَكَاءَ فِي مَا رَزَقْنَاكُمْ فَأَنْتُمْ فِيهِ سَوَاءٌ تَخَافُونَهُمْ كَخِيفَتِكُمْ أَنْفُسَكُمْ كَذَلِكَ نُفَصِّلُ الْآيَاتِ لِقَوْمٍ يَعْقِلُونَ ﴾

قدمت هذه الآية مثلا الغرض منه إبطال الشرك وإثبات وحدانية الله وتفرده بالخلق والرزق. حيث شبهت الهيئة المنتزعة من زعم المشركين أنَّ أصنامهم شركاء لله في التصرف ودافعون عن أولياءهم ما يريده الله تعالى من عقابٍ ونحوه- مع اعترافهم بأن هذه الأصنام مخلوقة لله تعالى.

شبهت هذه الهيئة بهيئة قوم لهم عبيدٌ صاروا شركاء في أرزاق سادتهم وساووهم في الكلمة والسطوة حتى صار سادتهم يحذرون منهم إذا أرادوا أن يتصرفوا في تلك الأرزاق أن يكونَ التصرفُ غيرَ مُرضٍ لعبيدهم. وهذه الهيئة الأخيرة غير مقبولة عقلاً- لدى المُخاطبين- إذ لا يتصور أن يحجر المملوك على تصرف سيده وأن يساويه فأثبت لهم بذلك خطأهم في تسوية أصنامهم بالله تعالى مع اعترافهم بأنها مخلوقة له.

The subtleties of this parable include:

(1) It is a comparison comprising complementary elements. It is possible to compare one complex state of affairs with another even when there are elements and parts missing from the comparison; but in this parable, despite it being a comparison between complex state of affairs, the elements can be taken individually, because they correspond both fully and equally to their counterparts.

These elements are as follows: [i] The Master of all creation corresponds to those who own slaves. [ii] The idols which are His creations correspond to the slaves whom those masters own. [iii] The partnership of the idols in the Creator's dominion and power corresponds to the partnership of the slaves in their masters' property. [iv] Their claim that God will sometimes refrain from acting on His will on those idols' account corresponds to the idea that those masters would be careful of the rights of their slaves when disposing of their own property, lest they should dispose of it in a way that would displease those slaves.

(2) The comparison provides a refutation to any argument for the worship of things other than God, because if all things other than God are not fit for such a partnership then they have no power or mastery, and so they lack the magnitude of status that would make them worthy objects of worship. No benefit can be hoped from them, since they possess no dominion, nor do they have any power or authority, for they are mere chattels, and a chattels has no power over anything.

(3) The verse concludes aptly with the words, *for rational people*, because these arguments only work in the absence of prideful obstinacy and wrongheadedness. If the matter remains unclear after all that has been said, this is a sign of irrationality, intellectual dishonesty, and disregard for evident proof.

ومن اللطائف المتعلقة بهذا التشبيه:

(١) أنه تشبيهٌ مُتكامل الأركان فقد تُشَبَّهُ هيئة بهيئة في مجموعها مع نقص في عناصر التشبيه وأجزاءه، لكن هذا التشبيه مع كونه تشبيه مجموع هيئة بهيئة أخرى إلا أنَّ أجزاء التشبيهِ صالحةٌ للتفريق لتمامها وتساويها مع نظائرها.

فيمكن تشبيه [١] مالك الخلق كلهم بالذين يملكون عبيدا [٢] وتشبيه الأصنام التي هي مخلوقة له تعالى بمماليك الناس [٣] وتشبيه تشريك الأصنام في التصرف مع الخالق في ملكه وسلطانه بتشريك العبد في التصرف في أرزاق سادتهم [٤] وتشبيه زعمهم عدول الله عن بعض ما يريد لأجل تلك الأصنام بحذر أصحاب الأرزاق التصرف في حظوظ عبيدهم تصرفا لا يرضى هؤلاء العبيد.

(٢) أنه بهذا التشبيه نفى جميع وجوه حسن العبادة عن الغير لأن الأغيار إذا لم يصلحوا للشركة فليس لهم مُلكٌ ولا مِلكٌ فلا عظمة لهم تدعو لعبادتهم ولا منفعة ترجى لعدم ملكهم وليس لهم قوة أو قدرة لأنهم مملوكون والمملوك لا يقدر على شيء.

(٣) أن الآية خُتمَت بما يناسب فقد قالت: "**لقوم يعقلون**" فإنما تنفع هذه الدلائل حيث انتفى العناد والمكابرة فإذا خفي الأمر بعد ذلك فإنما هو دليل انتفاء العقل ومجاوزة العدل ومخالفة الحجة الظاهرة.

(٤) ثم إن استخدام كلمة "نفصل" فيها معنى دقيق حيث إن

(4) The word "detail" here is also precisely chosen, because the parable clarifies and summarizes the meaning perfectly, leaving no room for argument or excuse, which is the purpose of going into precise detail. Hence a statement following which there can be no further argument or excuse is called in Arabic *faṣl al-khiṭāb* (a decisive statement). To detail (*tafṣīl*) means to elucidate (*tabyīn*).

المثل هنا أوضح ولخص الكلام غاية التلخيص حتى لم يترك حجة لمدعٍ ولا عذراً لمعتذرٍ وذلك هو الغرض من التفصيل. ولذا يقال للكلام الذي لا تبقي بعده شائبة حجة ولا عذر "فصل الخطاب" والتفصيل هو التبيين.

Parable 32: The Illuminating Lamp
Sūrat al-Aḥzāb (33), Verse 46

And as a summoner to God by His leave,
and as an illuminating lamp.

This verse compares the Prophet ﷺ to an illuminating lamp, the common element being the clear guidance that exists in both. A lit lamp dispels the darkness of a place so that none remains; and likewise, the noble person of the Prophet ﷺ and the guidance he brought dispel the ways of corruption and alteration, banish the means of error and misguidance, and show clearly the road to salvation and triumph.

The lamp is described as illuminating, even though illumination is already one of the essential properties of a lamp. This is an example of describing a thing by using an adjective derived from the word for it for the purpose of emphasis, such as how we might say, "this is a poet's poetry", "the knowledge of a knower", "the kindness of a kind man", or how one might describe a night (*layl*) as *alyal*, meaning very dark.

The many subtleties of this verse and its parable include:

(1) God likens the Prophet ﷺ to a lamp rather than to the sun, though the sun is brighter than a lamp, for several reasons. One is that the sun's light is not used to kindle other lights, unlike a lamp from which many lights can be kindled, just as the Companions

المثلُ الثاني والثلاثين: السِّراجُ المُنير
سورةُ الأحزاب الآية (٤٦)

﴿ وَدَاعِيًا إِلَى اللَّهِ بِإِذْنِهِ وَسِرَاجًا مُنِيرًا ﴾

تحتوي هذه الآية على تشبيه للنبي ﷺ بالسراج المنير ووجه الشبه الهداية الواضحة في كلٍّ. فكما أنَّ السراج الوقاد يزيل ظلمة المكان ولا يبقي لها باقية، كذلك شخصه الشريف ﷺ وما جاء به من الهدى يزيل مسالك التحريف والتبديل، ويزيح أسباب الضلالة والغي، ويوضح السبيل للنجاة والفوز.

ووصف السراج بأنه منيرٌ مع كون الإنارة لازما من لوازم السراج أصلا، من باب وصف الشيء بالوصف المشتق منه لإفادة قوة المعنى كما نقول: هذا "شعر شاعر" و "علم عالم" و "كرم كريم" وكما يقال: "ليلُ أليلُ" أي شديد الظلمة.

وفي الآية وما فيها من تشبيهٍ وتمثيل لطائف عديدة:

(١) أنه تعالى مثله ﷺ بالسراج ولم يمثله بالشمس مع أن الشمس أشد إضاءة من السراج وذلك لفوائد عدة منها: أن الشمس لا يؤخذ من نورها شيء بينما يؤخذ من نور السراج

of the Prophet ﷺ took from his light. That is why he called them stars, since the light of the stars, too, is not used to kindle other lights. Likewise, after the Companions were gone, the Followers and those who came after them took from the light of the Prophet ﷺ, which is the reference point for every *mujtahid* [qualified exponent of scholarly opinion]. The lights of the *mujtahids* are all from the Illuminating Lamp, the Bringer of Good News and of Warning ﷺ, and the stars continue to symbolize the superiority of Companionship. Had the Prophet ﷺ made them lamps, then all who came after them would have been allowed to choose whatever opinion to follow he pleased. But his ﷺ word and deed is the primary text, and anything else is merely an informed judgment (*ijtihād*) which may be bolstered by the status of the one who held it, if he was a person of nearness and attachment [to the Prophet ﷺ].

(2) In my view, the meaning of the illuminating lamp was fully realized in the Prophet ﷺ, for he showed the mind the path of God, removing from it the darknesses of unbelief, doubt, folly, and delusion; and he showed us the path of thankfulness, removing from it the darknesses of ingratitude, thanklessness, defiance, and treachery; and he showed us the path of virtues, removing from it the darknesses of vice, indecency, evil, transgression, and enmity. That was how he ﷺ was described in the Torah, according to the narration of al-Bukhārī from ʿAbd Allāh ibn ʿAmr ibn al-ʿĀṣ ؓ, who said: "He said in the Torah, 'O Prophet, We have sent you as a witness, a tiding-bearer, a warner, and a sanctuary for the Gentiles. You are My servant and My Emissary. I have called you the Totally Reliant One, who is not callous, nor rude, nor loud-mouthed in the marketplace; and who does not repay evil with evil but pardons and forgives...'"[37]

37: Bukhārī, *Ṣaḥīḥ* 4838.

أنوار كثيرة وكذلك أصحابه صلوات الله عليه وسلامه مأخوذون من نوره ولذلك قال في حقهم أنهم نجوم والنجم لا يؤخذ منه نور، وكذلك الصحابي إذا ذهب وغاب فالتابعي ومن دونه يستفيد من نور النبي ﷺ وكذلك مردُّ كل مجتهد. فأنوار المجتهدين كلها من السراج المنير والبشير النذير ﷺ. ويبقى فضل الصحبة للنجوم. ولو جعلهم النبي ﷺ سرجا لكان من بعدهم مُخير في أن يتبع أي قول شاء، لكن قوله ﷺ نص وفعله نصٌ وما دون ذلك اجتهاد يُستأنس بصاحبه إن كان ذا قرب وصلة.

(٢) قلت: ومعنى السراج المنير متحقق فيه ﷺ تمام التحقيق حيث عرَّفَ العقلَ طريقَ اللهِ فأزالَ عنه ظلماتِ الكفرِ والشكِّ والسخافةِ والوهمِ وعرّفَ الإنسانَ طريقَ الشُّكرِ فأزاحَ عنه ظلماتِ الكفران والجحودِ والعقوقِ والخيانةِ وعرَّفه طريق الفضائلِ فأزاح عنه ظلمات الرذيلة والفحشاء والمنكر والبغي والعدوان وقد جاء مثل ذلك في وصفه ﷺ في التوراة الذي رواه البخاري من حديث عبد الله بن عمرو بن العاص رضي الله عنهما قال: "قال في التوراة يا أيها النبي إنا أرسلناك شاهدا ومبشرا ونذيرا وحرزا للأميين أنت عبدي ورسولي سميتك المتوكل ليس بفظٍ ولا غليظٍ ولا سخَّابٍ في الأسواق ولا يدفعُ السيئة بالسيئةِ ولكن يعفو ويصفح."

Parable 33: In the Service of Partners

Sūrat al-Zumar (39), Verse 29

God has set forth a parable: a man shared by several quarrelling partners, and a man belonging exclusively to one man. Are the two equal in likeness? Praise be to God! But most of them do not know.

This verse depicts the state of the idolater who worships several gods, his mind divided among them and his worship vacillating; if he pleases one of his gods, he might anger the rest. His reason is dispersed, his state disturbed. He does not know which of them to rely upon or from which of them to seek help. The verse likens him to a slave owned by several partners, who will inevitably disagree and differ. They will assign different tasks to him and send him off this way and that on errands to meet their respective needs. He will be bewildered, unable to please them all, worn out by his attempts to do his duty to them, never having a moment's rest or a break. And if he ever has need of them for anything important, each will send him to another, and he will never get what he needs. He will not know where to turn, nor achieve his aim.

This comparison is then contrasted with another which depicts the state of the monotheist Muslim, who does as God commands him and turns to Him alone in hope of His approval, content in his mind and at peace in his heart. The verse likens him to a slave who is owned by a single master whom he serves exclusively, knowing

المثلُ الثالث والثلاثين: في خدمةٍ الشركاء
سورةُ الزمر الآية (٢٩)

﴿ ضَرَبَ اللَّهُ مَثَلًا رَجُلًا فِيهِ شُرَكَاءُ مُتَشَاكِسُونَ وَرَجُلًا سَلَمًا لِرَجُلٍ هَلْ يَسْتَوِيَانِ مَثَلًا الْحَمْدُ لِلَّهِ بَلْ أَكْثَرُهُمْ لَا يَعْلَمُونَ ﴾

مثّلَتْ هذه الآيةُ حالَ المُشركِ الذي يعْبُدُ آلهةً شتى فيتقسمُ عقله بينها وتردد عبادَتُهُ - إنْ أرضى أحدَ آلهتِهِ لعلهُ يُغضبُ الباقينَ- ففهمهُ شُعَاعٌ وحَالُهُ أوْزاعٌ لا يدري على أيهم يعتمدُ وبأيهم يَعتَضِدُ- بحالِ مملوكٍ اشتركَ فيه مالكونَ كثيرون لا يخلو حالُهُم من اختلافٍ وتنازعٍ فهم يطلبونه في مهنٍ شتى، ويَتَدافَعونهُ في حوائجهم وهو مُتَحيّرٌ في أمره لا يستطيع إرضاءهم، مُتْعَبٌ في أداءِ حقوقهم لا يستقيل لحظةً ولا يتمكنُ من استراحةٍ، وإنْ احتاجَهُم في مُهِمّ، ردّهُ كلُّ واحد إلى الآخر فلا يُدركُ حاجته، ولا يعرفُ وُجهته ولا يُحَصّلُ بُغيَتَه.

ويقابل هذا التمثيلَ، تمثيل حال المسلم الموحّدِ الذي يقوم بما أمره الله به ويتوجه إليه وحده مؤملا رضاه مستقر البال مطمئن الفؤاد بحال العبد المملوك الخالص لمالكٍ ومخدومٍ

his master's will. His mind is at one, his heart is composed, and his situation is stable.

The purpose of this parable and comparison is to illustrate the vileness of idolatry and the beauty of monotheism, for any rational person will see that the condition of the slave who serves a single master is better, nobler, and sounder than the state of the one over whom a group of masters compete, each having their own desires and particular concerns.

The subtleties of the verse include:

(1) The verse alludes to the rivalry between the idols which is claimed or affirmed by those who worship them. Those who believe in many gods, even if they be idols, assert that each one of them has a particular power and authority. For instance, they might say that Saturn has a certain power while Jupiter has another, and that there is a fertility god and a sterility god, and that this conflict is always raging between the gods because of the appetites, attributes, quarrels, and rivalries which they attribute to them, which causes the worshiper always to be confused about them, his mind never being at ease.

(2) The verse introduces the parable in the past tense in order to narrow the gap between the present and the past for the purpose of arousing interest and implying that the occurrence of the thing is certain. According to al-Zamakhsharī,[38] actually the past tense here is meant in the sense of a command, and it means, "Set forth to them a parable." The command is worded as a statement as a way of alluding to the truth of the Prophet's ﷺ knowledge.

38: Maḥmūd ibn 'Umar al-Zamakhsharī (d. 538/1144) of Khwarazm was a theologian and commentator on the Qur'ān. His commentary *al-Kashshāf* is especially valued for its linguistic analysis.

واحدٍ يخدمه على سبيل الإخلاص، يعرفُ مرادَ سيده ففهمه واحدٌ وقلبه مجتمعٌ وأمره مستقرٌ.

والغرضُ من هذا التمثيل والمقارنة تقبيح الشركِ وتحسينُ التوحيدِ إذ إنَّ العاقل سيرى أن حال العبد الذي يخدمُ سيداً واحداً أفضلُ وأكرمُ وأقومُ مِنْ حالِ مَن يتنازعه جملة من الأرباب لكل واحدٍ منها مرادٌ أو تخصص.

وفي الآية لطائفُ ودقائقُ منها:

(١) أن الآية أشارت إلى ما يدعيه أو يثبته عُبّادُ تلك الأصنام من مشاكسةٍ بينها، فإنَّ من يُعدّدُ الآلهةَ- وإن كانت أصناما- يُثبتُ لكل واحدٍ منها سطوة وقوة فيقولون مثلاً: في زُحَلَ كذا وفي المشترى كذا وهذا إله الخصب وهذا إله الجدب ويظلُّ الصراه بين هذه الآلهة قائم لما نسبوا لها من شهواتٍ وصفاتٍ ومنازعاتٍ ومشاكساتٍ ويظلُّ العبدُ حائرا بينهم لا يقرُّ له بال.

(٢) أن الآية ساقت المثل بصيغة الفعل الماضي لتقريب زمن الحال من زمن الماضي بغرض التشويق والدلالة على تحقق الوقوع. وقال الزمخشري: بل هو بمعنى الأمر والمعنى "اضرب لهم مثلا" فالخبر بمعنى الأمر إشارة لصدق علمِ النبي ﷺ.

Parable 34: The Lifestyle of Livestock
Sūrat Muḥammad ﷺ (47), Verse 12

As for those who disbelieve, they enjoy themselves and eat as the livestock animals eat; and the Fire will be a home for them.

This verse compares the enjoyment of the unbelievers, who do not believe in the Hereafter and indulgence in the appetites and pleasures of the world, to the way that livestock eat and enjoy themselves. The unbeliever's aspiration is fixed on the world, and his heart is void of faith in the Day of Resurrection, and so he is interested in nothing more than his stomach and loins, and his only concern is to pursue the appetites of this present life. Yet since the duration of this life is so short, its enjoyments, however plentiful and precious they may seem in the eyes of their devotees, are few; and the benefit which a person receives from them, however much it may amount to, is trifling. Al-Zamakhsharī said: "It means that they benefit from the enjoyment of this world for a few days, and they consume mindlessly without thinking about the final end, just as livestock eat in their pastures and troughs, unaware that they will soon be slaughtered. The Fire will be [those people's] dwelling and station in the Hereafter."

Other subtle meanings of this verse include:

(1) God Most High does not attribute the word "home" to the pronoun by saying, "their home", but rather avoids this and uses the

المثلُ الرابع والثلاثين: عيشةُ الأنعام
سورة محمد ﷺ الآية (١٢)

﴿ وَالَّذِينَ كَفَرُوا يَتَمَتَّعُونَ وَيَأْكُلُونَ كَمَا تَأْكُلُ الْأَنْعَامُ وَالنَّارُ مَثْوًى لَهُمْ ﴾

مثّلَتْ هذه الآيةُ تمتع الكافرين الذين لا يؤمنون بالآخرة وانتفاعهم بشهوات الدنيا ولذائذها بتمتع الأنعام وأكلها. وذلك لأن الكافر لما تعلقت همته بالدنيا وخلا قلبه عن الإيمان بيوم القيامة، صار همه بطنه وفرجه، وحظهُ متابعةُ شهوات هذه الحياة الدنيا. ولما كانت مدة هذه الدنيا قصيرة وأمدُها ضيّقٌ كان متاعها - مهما كثر وغَلا في عين أهليه - قليلٌ وحظ صاحبها من النفع - بالغاً ما بلغ- بخس. قال الزمخشري: المرادُ أنهم ينتفعون بمتاع هذه الدنيا أياما قلائل ويأكلون غافلين غير مفكرين في العاقبة كما تأكل الأنعام في مسارحها ومعالفها غافلة عما هي بصدده من النحر، والنار منزلهم ومقامهم في الآخرة.

ومما يتصل بهذه الآية من المعاني الدقيقة:

(١) أن الله تعالى لم يُضف الضمير إلى كلمة (مثوى) فلم يقل: والنار مثواهم بل عدلَ عن ذلك إلى التعليق باللام

preposition "for", which is usually implicit in the possessive construction. This allows, by the use of the indefinite article preceding the word "home" (or in Arabic, the *tanwīn* in *mathwan*), the evocation of a sense of being firmly settled in the Fire, as though he were saying, "the Fire will be a sturdy home for them." That is because the tiding of the Fire precedes the seeing of it here, and therefore He wishes to emphasize it; but that is not necessary when He says, *He will say, "The Fire is your home"* [Qur'ān 6:128], because that statement will be made at the Resurrection, when they can see the Fire.

(2) The purpose of this verse is not to compare the unbelievers to livestock animals, as some people might suppose at first glance. The purpose is to depict the attachment to food, drink, and other appetites, despite their impermanence and transience, of those who do not believe in God and the Hereafter, along with their obliviousness to the terrible punishment which awaits them, by comparing this to how cattle enjoy food and other appetites and think of nothing else.

The comparison here centers on the obliviousness to consequences and the failure to differentiate between what is harmful and what is not, such as consuming unlawful substances and not being careful to avoid them, or consuming beyond the limits of need and the proper time. The believer is restricted, in what he eats and enjoys, by the edicts of the lawful and the forbidden (*ḥalāl* and *ḥarām*) and by the laws of necessity. He may not eat more than he needs, or eat all the time, or consume what is not lawful for him. A hadith related by al-Bukhārī and Muslim states that the unbeliever eats in seven stomachs, but the believer ought to make do with a little.[39] Al-Tirmidhī narrated the hadith, "No human being ever filled a worse container than his own stomach."[40]

(3) It has occurred to me that another aspect of this comparison is that unbelievers are oblivious to matters relating to the enjoyment

39: Bukhārī, *Ṣaḥīḥ* 462; Muslim, *Ṣaḥīḥ* 1764.
40: *Sunan* 2380.

التي شأنها أن تُنوى في الإضافة؛ وذلك ليفيدَ بوجودِ التنوين في كلمةِ (مثوىً) معنى التمكن من القرار في النار. فكأنه قال: والنار مثوىً قويا لهم. وذلك لأن الإخبار عن النار هنا حصل قبل مشاهدتها فأراد التأكيد بينما لم يحتج إلى ذلك في قوله: "قال النارُ مثواكم" (الأنعام: ١٢٨) لأنه إخبار عنها وهم يشاهدونها في المحشر.

(٢) ليس المراد من الآية تشبيه الكافرين بالأنعام كما قد يتبادر إلى ذهن البعض. وإنما المراد تمثيل التعلق بالمطاعم والمشارب والشهوات مع بقاءها إلى حين وزوالها عن قريب عند من لا يؤمن بالله واليوم الآخر مع غفلته عما هو مقدم عليه من عذاب شديد بحال تمتع الأنعام بالمطعوم والشهوة وعدم تفكيرها فيما دون ذلك. فالتشبيه هنا من جهة الغفلةِ عن تدبير العاقبة وعدم تمييز المضرِّ من غيره كأكلِ الحرام وعدم توقيه وكذا كونه غير مقصور على الحاجة ولا على وقتها. والمؤمنُ محكومٌ فيما يأكلُ ويشتهي بمعالم الحلال والحرام وأحكام الحاجة فلا يأكلُ فوق حاجته ولا في كلِّ وقتٍ ولا مما لا يجوز له. وقد ورد في حديث البخاري ومسلم أن الكافر يأكل في سبعة أمعاءٍ والمؤمنُ يكتفي بما تيسر. وفي الخبر الذي أخرجه الترمذي: "ما ملأ آدميٌّ وعاء شرا من بطنه."

(٣) وقعَ في الخاطر أنَّ مِن وجوهِ هذا التشبيه غياب الكافر عما يتعلق بالتمتع بالشهوات - ومنها الأكل- من الآداب التي ربطها بها الشارع الشريف. فما من شهوةٍ ولا فعلٍ إلا

of appetites, including eating, such as the rules of conduct which the Noble Law-Giver has assigned to them. Every appetite, and every act, has been assigned rules of conduct by the Law-Giver which lead to higher states of being and differentiate human from beast. The human being shares the basic appetites of eating, drinking, and sex in common with livestock animals, but he has been distinguished by the rules of conduct which God has enjoined upon him for before and after eating, and before and after sex, in addition to giving thanks for them, not violating their prohibition when they are not legally accessible, and seeking divine reward by engaging in them, so that they are not sought merely for their own sake, nor permanently fixated upon. All of this can be learned from the conduct of the Message-Bringer ﷺ, and so anyone who does not become attached to that heaven-sent Prophet ﷺ, and who does not benefit from that heaven-sent guidance, will continue to enjoy those appetites which he shares in common with the cattle, even if the image appears different or the foodstuffs are not the same. That is what the comparison means, so be aware of this.

(4) The scholars say that the consumption of food is an important subject which requires many branches of knowledge to be done correctly, so that food is used as an aid for study and piety, and one does not let oneself gorge freely like a beast in the field. Shaykh ʿAllāma Muḥammad ibn ʿAbd al-Raḥīm al-Mullā al-Aḥsāʾī (d. 1100/1688) says in his book *Miftāḥ al-qurb fī sharḥ manẓūmat Ādāb al-akl wal-shurb*:

> The lights of religion are none other than its courtesies and customs, which the servant [of God] ought to be bridled by and the pious man ought to be bound by, so that he may weigh the appetite for food in the balance of the Law whether indulging it or denying it. That will make it a means of preventing sin and earning reward, even if a trace

وربطه الشارع بآداب مرعية تنتج أحوالا سنية وتفرق بين الإنسان والبهيمة. فالإنسان يشترك في أصل شهوة الأكل والشرب والفرج مع الأنعام لكنه يتميز بما أمره الله تعالى به من آداب قبل الطعام وبعده، وقبل الجماع وبعده فضلا عن الشكر عليها وعدم تعدي حرمتها عند تعذر تحصيلها، وطلب الثواب بفعلها فلا هي مُتَغيّاةٌ لذاتها ولا مُتَعلَّقٌ بها تعلقا أبديا. وكلُّ ذلك مستفاد من سلوك صاحب الرسالة صلوات الله وسلامه عليه؛ فمَن لم يتعلق بهذا النبي المبعوث ﷺ ومن لم ينتفع بهذا الهدى المبثوث بقيَ له من التمتع بالشهوات المشترك بينه وبين الأنعام وإن اختلفت الصورة أو تباينت المطاعم فكان هذا وجه التشبيه، فتفَطّن.

(٤) ذكر العلماء أن تناول الطعام أصلُ كبير يحتاج إلى علوم كثيرة كي يحصل المطلوب؛ من الاستعانة بالأكل على العلم والتقوى ولا يترك المرء نفسه مسترسلا استرسال البهائم في المرعى. قال الشيخ العلامة محمد بن عبد الرحيم الملا الأحسائي (ت ١١٠٠ هـ) في كتابه (مفتاح القرب في شرح منظومة آداب الأكل والشرب):

> وإنما أنوار الدين آدابه وسننه التي يُزَمُّ العبد بزمامها ويُلجَمُ المتقي بلجامها حتى يزن بميزان الشرع شهوة الطعام في إقدامها وإحجامها، فتصير بسببها مدفعةً في الوزر ومجلبة للأجر وإن كان فيها أدنى حظ للنفس. قال النبي ﷺ: "إنَّ الرجلَ ليؤجرَ في اللقمة

of self-interest remains in it. The Prophet ﷺ said, "A man will certainly be rewarded for the morsel of food which he lifts to his mouth, and to his wife's mouth" (Bukhārī, from a narration of Abū Sa'īd). The Proof of Islam al-Ghazālī, may God benefit us through him, said that this only applies when he lifts the morsel by the religion and for the religion, observing its courtesies, customs, and duties.

يرفعها إلى فيه وإلى فيّ أمرأته." (البخاري من حديث سعد) قال الحجة الغزالى - نفعنا الله به- في ذلك: وإنما ذلك إذا رفعها بالدين وللدين مراعيا آدابه وسننه ووظائفه. ا.ه

Parable 35: Like a Sapling that Grows Stout

Sūrat al-Fatḥ (48), Verse 29

Their likeness in the Gospel is as a sapling that puts forth its shoot and strengthens it, so it grows stout and rises firmly upon its stalk, delighting the sowers, that through them He may enrage the disbelievers. To those of them who believe and do righteous deeds, God has promised forgiveness and an immense reward.

This verse likens the Messenger of God ﷺ and his Companions, who had the honor of being with him and the felicity of his company, to a sapling which emerges from the grain in a feeble state but then grows to the limit of perfection, its stalk thickening and its fruits coming forth in abundance, until it is firmly established. This evokes how the religion of Islam began weak but grew stronger day by day until it became thoroughly established and overcame its enemies.

This is a parable which can be analyzed and each of the separate comparisons considered in turn. Our master Muḥammad ﷺ is represented by the sapling, and the believers by the seeds of the plant which it disperses into the earth, such as [early converts like] Abū Bakr, Khadīja, ʿAlī, and ʿAmmār. The shoot represents those who aided the Muslims; at first when he ﷺ called to God all by himself, few people joined him, but then God Most High strengthened him with additional followers. The verse then makes clear what the purpose of the comparison is, and the wise purpose of establishing them in that state of growth, ascension, and strength: to enrage the

المثلُ الخامس والثلاثين: كزرعٍ استغلظ فاستوى
سورةُ الفتح الآية (٢٩)

﴿ وَمَثَلُهُمْ فِي الْإِنْجِيلِ كَزَرْعٍ أَخْرَجَ شَطْأَهُ فَآزَرَهُ فَاسْتَغْلَظَ فَاسْتَوَى عَلَى سُوقِهِ يُعْجِبُ الزُّرَّاعَ لِيَغِيظَ بِهِمُ الْكُفَّارَ وَعَدَ اللَّهُ الَّذِينَ آمَنُوا وَعَمِلُوا الصَّالِحَاتِ مِنْهُمْ مَغْفِرَةً وَأَجْرًا عَظِيمًا ﴾

مثّلَتْ هذه الآيةُ رسول الله ﷺ وأصحابه الذين فازوا بمعيته وسعدوا بصحبته بالزرع الذي يخرج ضعيفا من الحبّةِ ثم ينمو إلى حدِّ الكمال ويغلظ عوده ويكثر ثمره حتى يستحكم. وذلك يتضمن تشبيه بدء دين الإسلام ضعيفا وتقويه يوما فيوما حتى استحكم أمره وتغلب على أعدائه.

وهذا التمثيل قابل لاعتبار تجزئة التشبيه في أجزاءه بأن يُشبه سيدنا محمد ﷺ بالزارع ويشبَّه المؤمنون بحبات الزرع التي يبذرها في الأرض مثل أبي بكر وخديجة وعليٍّ وعمار والشطء بِمَن أيدوا المسلمين، إذ إنه صلوات الله وسلامه عليه دعا إلى الله وحده وانضم إليه نفر قليل ثم قواه الله تعالى بمن انضم إليه. وبينت الآية غرض التمثيل والحكمة في أقامتهم بتلك الحالة من النماء والترقية في

unbelievers when they see how well the believers are faring and how their tide is rising, despite their violent enmity and opposition to them.

Al-Qurṭubī[41] quotes Abū ʿUrwa al-Zubayrī: "We were with Mālik ibn Anas[42] when they told him of a man who spoke ill of the Companions of the Messenger of God ﷺ. Mālik recited this verse up to the Words, *that through them He may enrage the disbelievers*, then said, 'This verse is aimed at anybody who harbors in his heart rage at any of the Companions of God's Messenger ﷺ.'"

Other subtleties of this blessed verse include:

(1) The allusion to this being their description in the Gospel agrees with the many allusions to crops in the Gospels, such as the Gospel of Matthew 13, verses 3-9: "Then He spoke many things to them in parables, saying: 'Behold, a sower went out to sow. And as he sowed, some seed fell by the wayside; and the birds came and devoured them. Some fell on stony places, where they did not have much earth; and they immediately sprang up because they had no depth of earth. But when the sun was up they were scorched, and because they had no root they withered away. And some fell among thorns, and the thorns sprang up and choked them. But others fell on good ground and yielded a crop: some a hundredfold, some sixty, some thirty. He who has ears to hear, let him hear!'"

(2) The verse alludes to the growth of faith in their hearts, and the visible effects which they were having, such as the many converts to God's religion, and how the foundation of this is mutual support, cooperation, and the brotherhood of faith, which is the firmest of ties of faith and the most manifest sign of Islam.

41: Muḥammad ibn Aḥmad al-Qurṭubī (d. 671/1273) was a renowned exegete and jurist of Andalusia, and author of one of the most highly regarded Qur'ān commentaries.

42: Mālik ibn Anas (d. 179/795), a hadith narrator and jurist, was the founder of the Mālikī school of Sunni jurisprudence.

الزيادة والقوة وهي إغاظة الكفار لما يرونه من صلاح حالهم وظهور أمرهم بالرغم من شدة العداء والمُحادّة لهم.

قال القرطبي: قال أبو عروة الزبيري كنا عند مالك بن أنس فذكروا عنده رجلا ينتقص أصحاب رسول الله ﷺ فقرأ مالك هذه الآية إلى أن بلغ قوله تعالى: "**لِيَغِيظَ بِهِمُ الْكُفَّار**" فقال: من أصبح من الناس في قلبه غيظ على أحدٍ من أصحاب رسول الله ﷺ فقد أصابته هذه الآية.

ومن لطائف هذه الآية الكريمة:

(١) أن إشارتها إلى أن هذا هو وصفهم في الأنجيل يتفق مع ورود كثير من الإشارات للزرع في الأنجيل فقد جاء في إنجيل متى الإصحاح ١٣ الفقرة ٣ - ٩: "هُوَذَا الزَّارِعُ قَدْ خَرَجَ لِيَزْرَعَ، وَفِيمَا هُوَ يَزْرَعُ سَقَطَ بَعْضٌ عَلَى الطَّرِيقِ، فَجَاءَتِ الطُّيُورُ وَأَكَلَتْهُ. وَسَقَطَ آخَرُ عَلَى الأَمَاكِنِ الْمُحْجِرَةِ، حَيْثُ لَمْ تَكُنْ لَهُ تُرْبَةٌ كَثِيرَةٌ، فَنَبَتَ حَالاً إِذْ لَمْ يَكُنْ لَهُ عُمْقُ أَرْضٍ. وَلكِنْ لَمَّا أَشْرَقَتِ الشَّمْسُ احْتَرَقَ، وَإِذْ لَمْ يَكُنْ لَهُ أَصْلٌ جَفَّ. وَسَقَطَ آخَرُ عَلَى الشَّوْكِ، فَطَلَعَ الشَّوْكُ وَخَنَقَهُ. وَسَقَطَ آخَرُ عَلَى الأَرْضِ الْجَيِّدَةِ فَأَعْطَى ثَمَرًا، بَعْضٌ مِئَةً وَآخَرُ سِتِّينَ وَآخَرُ ثَلاَثِينَ. مَنْ لَهُ أُذُنَانِ لِلسَّمْعِ، فَلْيَسْمَعْ."

(٢) أنَّ الآية تشير إلى نماء الإيمان في قلوبهم وظهور آثارهم من تكثير الداخلين في دين الله وأنَّ أساس ذلك التآزر والتعاضد والأخوة الإيمانية التي هي أوثق عرى الإيمان وأظهرُ مظاهر الإسلام.

Parable 36: The Backbiter

Sūrat al-Ḥujurāt (49), Verse 12

Would any of you like to eat the flesh of his dead brother? You would detest it.

This verse likens backbiting, which means speaking of a person in their absence in a way they would not like, to consuming the flesh of a dead person who cannot defend himself. It is only backbiting if nothing is said which impugns the person's honor; but if such a thing is said, it crosses the bounds of backbiting into outright defamation and slander.

The question in the verse is rhetorical, because of course no one would like to do such a thing. Backbiting has always been prevalent among people, and is one of the most serious blemishes of the tongue which have grave dangers and consequences.

This comparison can be separated into its constituent parts. The backbiter is represented by the flesh-eater, the victim by the brother. The victim's absence from the gathering where the backbiting occurs is represented by death, because they both signify absence and inability to defend oneself.

The lessons of the verse include:

(1) It indicates the unlawfulness of backbiting, which is established by narrations from the Sunna as well as the prohibition issued here. One such narration is the one in which the Prophet ﷺ said,

المثلُ السادس والثلاثين: مثالُ المُغتاب
سورةُ الحجرات الآية (١٢)

﴿ أَيُحِبُّ أَحَدُكُمْ أَنْ يَأْكُلَ لَحْمَ أَخِيهِ مَيْتًا فَكَرِهْتُمُوهُ ﴾

مثّلَتْ هذه الآيةُ حالة الغِيبةِ - وهي ذكر أحد غائب بما لا يحب أن يُذكَر به- بحالة أكل لحم المرء وهو ميت لا يدافع عن نفسه. والغيبة إنما تكون إن لم يُذكر ما يثلمُ العِرض، فإذا ذكر ما يثلم العرض، خرجت من كونها غيبة إلى كونها قذعا وقذفا.

والاستفهام في الآية تقريري لتحقق معنى أن كلَّ أحدٍ لا يحب ذلك. وقد كانت الغيبة ولا تزال فاشية في الناس وقد عُدَّت من آفات اللسان العظيم خطرها وأثرها.

وهذا التشبيه قابل للتفريق في أجزاءه، بأن يُشبَّه الذي اغتاب بآكل اللحم والذي اغتيب بأخٍ وتشبيه غيبته عن المجلس الذي يغتاب فيه بالموت لأنها تحمل معنى الانقطاع وعدم إمكان دفاعه عن نفسه.

وفي الآية فوائد منها:

أنها دلّت على حرمة الغيبة وقد ثبتت حرمتها بآثار من

"Do you know what backbiting is?" They replied, "God and His Messenger know best." He said, "It is mentioning your brother in a way he would dislike." Someone said, "What if what I say about my brother is true?" He replied, "If what you say about him is true, you have backbitten him. If what you say is not true, you have slandered him."[43]

Another hadith says, "All of a Muslim is sacrosanct to his fellow Muslim: his blood, his wealth, and his honor."[44] Mālikīs consider it to be a major sin (*kabīra*), the Shāfiʿīs a minor one (*ṣaghīra*). Regarding this subject and the importance of holding one's tongue, ʿAbd al-Wāḥid Ibn ʿĀshir[45] says:

> Close your eyes to forbidden sights,
> Avert your ears from sinful words:
> Backbiting, tattling, perjury, lies.
> Above all, your tongue must cause no harm!

Exceptions are made for criticizing witnesses and hadith narrators, and advice given regarding potential business partners or spouses, as long as the advice does not go beyond the bounds of what needs to be known about the person's character. Likewise, it is not backbiting to speak of a person's offenses if he is a flagrant, open sinner.

Once the Prophet ﷺ was told that ʿUyayna ibn Ḥiṣn was at the door asking permission to come in, and so he said, by way of warning those who could hear him, "A bad brother to his tribe!", because at that time he had deviated from Islam.

(2) The verse features a rhetorical style called antithesis (*ṭibāq*), which is a way of summarizing and clarifying the meaning and

43: Muslim, *Ṣaḥīḥ* 2589.

44: Muslim, *Ṣaḥīḥ* 2564.

45: ʿAbd al-Wāḥid Ibn ʿĀshir (d. 1040/1631) was a Moroccan scholar. His didactic poem *al-Murshid al-muʿīn* is an important primer in the Mālikī school.

السنة مع النهي عنها هنا. من تلك الآثار قوله ﷺ: أتدرون ما الغيبة؟ قالوا: "الله ورسوله أعلم." قال: "ذكرك أخاك بما يكره." قيل: "أفرأيت إن كان في أخي ما أقول؟" قال: "إن كانَ فيه ما تقولُ فقد اغتبته، وإنْ لم يكن فيه ما تقول، فقد بَهتَّه." (رواه مسلم عن أبي هريرة) وفي الحديث الآخر: "كلُّ المسلم على المسلم حرام، دمه وماله وعرضه." (رواه مسلم والترمذي) وقد عَدَّها سادتنا المالكية من الكبائر وعدها السادة الشافعية من الصغائر. وفي هذا المعنى وأهمية حفظ اللسان يقول عبد الواحد بن عاشر:

يَغُضُّ عينه عَن المَحَارِمِ
يكُفُّ سَمعَهُ عَن المَآثِمِ
كَغِيبَةٍ نَمِيمَةٍ زُورٍ كَذِبْ
لِسَانُهُ أَحرَى بِترِكِ مَا جُلِبْ

وقد استثني من ذلك تجريح الشهود ورواة الحديث وما يقالُ للمستشير في مخالطةٍ أو مصاهرةٍ بشرط ألا يتجاوز الحد الذي يحصل به وصف الحالة المسؤول عنها. وكذلك لا غيبة لفاسق بذكر فسقه وقد قال النبي ﷺ حين استؤذِنَ عنده لعُيينةَ بن حصن -ليُحَذِّر من سمعه: "بئس أخو العشيرة." إذ كان حينئذٍ منحرفا عن الإسلام.

(٢) اشتملت الآية على طباق والطباق أسلوب بلاغيٌ يُجَمِّلُ المعني ويوضحه ويساعد في ربط المعاني. والطباق في هذه الآية بين "**قوله أيحب**" و قوله "**فكرهتموه**". ولا شك أن التعبير عن

assisting in the linking of concepts. The antithesis here is between the words, *Would any of you like...?*, and the words, *You would detest it*. There is no doubt that referring to the victim of backbiting as *his brother* is a further allusion to the heinous and odious nature of the sin, because it is an offense against the brother, who has the right to be defended and protected from criticism in his absence.

المُغتاب بلفظ "أخيه" فيه إشارة إلى قبح الجريمة وفظاعتها إذ إنها عدوان على الأخ الذي حقه أن يدافع عنه وأن تُحفظَ غيبته وترد عيبته.

Parable 37: The Goodly Loan

Sūrat al-Ḥadīd (57), Verse 11

Who is it that will lend God a goodly loan, that He may multiply it for him, and that he may have a generous reward?

This verse likens a person who donates to God's cause to someone who gives a goodly loan, meaning one free of anything which would put the borrower under pressure, and which is given with a fully contented soul and a desire for reward in the Hereafter in both cases, as well as the loan being given from lawfully-earned wealth, and given eagerly.

The person who donates to God's cause gives eagerly and lovingly, spending not for the sake of earning praise or fame, but rather to draw nearer to God Most High and out of attachment to earning His approval. Likewise, one who gives goodly loans to other people gives happily, with eagerness for virtue and generosity of soul.

Perhaps the common element between donator and lender is the generosity of their souls and the goodness of their natural dispositions. No one gives a loan in this way unless wealth is a trivial concern to him and he knows that its value lies in winning felicity in the Hereafter, so that he prefers the enduring future to the ephemeral present.

Likewise, no one spends for God's cause except the true believer, who knows what lies in store for him and thinks nothing of letting go of the trappings of the world.

المثلُ السابع والثلاثين: القرضُ الحَسَن
سورةُ الحديد الآية (١١)

﴿ مَنْ ذَا الَّذِي يُقْرِضُ اللَّهَ قَرْضًا حَسَنًا فَيُضَاعِفَهُ لَهُ وَلَهُ أَجْرٌ كَرِيمٌ ﴾

مثّلَتْ هذه الآيةُ المنفق في سبيل الله بالمُقرِض قرضاً حسنا - أي خاليا من كل ما يُضيّق على المُقتَرِض، بجامع كون نفس المقرض طيبة في كُلٍّ ورغبة المقرض في الحالين في الأجر الأُخروي فضلا عن كون كلا القرضين من حلال ووجود الرغبة في العطاء.

فالمنفق في سبيل الله يرغب في الإنفاق ويحبه ويبذل لا طلبا للمحمدة أو رغبة في الشهرة بل زلفى لله تعالى وتعلقا بمرضاته، وكذلك الذي يقرضُ الناس قرضا حسنا يعطي عن طيبِ خاطر ويبذل رغبة في الخير وسخاءً من النفس. قلت: ولعل وجه الشبه بين المنفق والمقرض سخاء نفسيهما وطيب عنصريهما؛ فلا يُقرض بهذا الطريقة إلا مَن هانَ عليه المال وعرفَ أنَّ قيمته في إسعاد الآخرين فآثر العاقبة على الفانية ولا ينفق في سبيل الله إلا المؤمن الصادق العارف بما هو مقبل عليه والعازف عما في يده من لَعَاعةِ الدنيا.

وفي الآية لطائف منها:

The subtleties of the verse include:

(1) The verse is phrased in the form of a question, its purpose being to provide encouragement and inspiration, which is more likely to foster a healthy rivalry and an eager competitive spirit for the sake of virtue and piety.

(2) One scholar said that a loan is only goodly (*ḥasan*) if it combines the following ten qualities: [i] It must be lawful. [ii] It must be given from good-quality possessions, not low-quality ones. [iii] It must be something that the giver feels reluctant to give away, because he would rather keep it. [iv] It must be donated to the most worthy recipient. [v] It must be kept secret. [vi] It must not be followed by demands for gratitude or abuse. [vii] It must be given for the sake of God's Countenance, not to show off. [viii] The giver must belittle and think nothing of what he gives, however valuable it may be. [ix] The donation must be from the giver's most prized possessions. [x] The giver must not aggrandize himself and disparage the recipient, but rather must do the opposite, and consider himself lucky for God having directed the needy person to him.

(3) God Most High affirms that the recompense for such a loan will be *a generous reward*, meaning the most precious of rewards, because the word *karīm* (generous, noble) means the most precious and grandest type of thing. Hence God the Exalted says in *Sūrat al-Naml*: *O chieftains, a noble letter has been delivered to me* [Qur'ān 27:29]. The word *karīm* is also used in Arabic to describe a stone which is precious.

(١) أنَّ الآية وردت بصيغة الاستفهام، والغرض منه الحضُّ والتحريض مجازا وهو أدعى إلى التنافس في الخير والمسارعة إلى البر.

(٢) قال بعض العلماء: إنما يكون القرض حسنا إن جمع أوصافا عشرةً؛ أولها [١]: أن يكون حلالا، وثانيها [٢]: أن يكون من أفضل المال دون الرديء، وثالثها [٣]: أن يتصدق المرء به وهو شحيح يحبه ويحتاجه، ورابعها[٤]: أن ينفقه في الأولى والخامس [٥]: أن يكتم نفقته، والسادس[٦]: أن لا يتبعها منّا ولا أذى، والسابع [٧]: أن يقصد به وجه الله لا الرياء، والثامن[٨]: أن يستحقرَ ويستَقِلَّ ما يعطي مهما كَثُرَ، والتاسع [٩]: أن يكون من أحب ماله إليه، والعاشر[٠١]: أن لا يرى عزَّ نفسه وذلَّ الفقير بل يرى العكس وأنّه محظوظ أنَّ الله أحال الفقير إليه.

(٣) أنَّ الله تعالى أثبت ثواب القرض على أنّهُ "أجرٌ كريمٌ" أي أنفس الأجور لأن الكريم من كل شيء هو أنفسه وأعظمه ومنها قوله سبحانه وتعالى في سورة النمل: "إني أُلقيَ إليَّ كِتابٌ كريمٌ" (النمل: ٢٩) ومنه قولهم للحجر النفيس، حجر كريم.

Parable 38: The Effects of Neglecting The Revealed Law

Sūrat al-Ḥadīd (57), Verse 16

They should not become like those who were given the Book before, but then a long time passed and their hearts were hardened.

This verse depicts what happens to believing hearts when they part with Revelation and stray from the laws of God and defy them, likening them to the hearts of the People of the Book which can no longer be considered pious or submissive, having abandoned their religion. The reason for that is that straying from the revealed Law, its people, and its rulings causes piety and reverence to leave the heart; once piety leaves the heart, it becomes hardened; and when the heart hardens, it dies, and counsel no longer has any impact upon it, nor does it retain any vestige of light. It is then that devils snatch it away, and base desires play with it.

Abandonment of the revealed Law with the passage of time means several things. One is abandonment of the Prophets, the present-day counterpart of which is avoidance of the religious scholars and the people of sincerity, for that inevitably leads to hardening of the heart. That is why the early Muslims, may God be well-pleased with them, used to got to look upon the faces of God's people so that their hearts would be softened. Ja'far ibn Sulaymān[46] said,

46: Ja'far ibn Sulaymān al-Ḍubā'ī (d. 178/795) was a hadith narrator of Basra.

المثلُ الثامن والثلاثين: آثارُ هجران الشرع
سورةُ الحديد الآية (١٦)

﴿ وَلَا يَكُونُوا كَالَّذِينَ أُوتُوا الْكِتَابَ مِن قَبْلُ فَطَالَ عَلَيْهِمُ الْأَمَدُ فَقَسَتْ قُلُوبُهُمْ ﴾

شبه في هذه الآية حال القلوب المؤمنة حين تهجر الوحي وتبتعد عن أحكام الله فتجترئُ عليها، بحال قلوب أهل الكتاب التي لم تعُد تخشع بعد مزاولتهم دينهم. وسبب ذلك أن الابتعاد عن الشرع وأهله وأحكامه يُذهبُ الخشية من القلب والتوقير وإذا ذهبت الخشية من القلب صار قاسيا، وإذا قسا القلب مات ولم تعد الموعظة تؤثر فيه ولم يبق فيه أثر النور فاحتوشته حينئذٍ الشياطين وتلاعبت به الأهواء.

والمرادُ من طول الأمد و هجران الوحي والابتعاد عنه أمور منها، الابتعاد عن الأنبياء ومثله اليوم البعد عن العلماء وأهل الصدق فإن ذلك يورث القسوة في القلب لا محالة ولذلك كان السلف -رضوان الله عليهم- يذهبون للنظر في وجوه أهل الله لتلين قلوبهم. قال جعفر بن سليمان: "كنتُ إذا وجدت من قلبي قسوة غدوت فنظرتُ إلى وجه محمد بن واسع كان كأنهُ ثكلى." وقال مالك بن

"Whenever I felt any hardness in my heart, I would go and look upon the face of Muḥammad ibn Wāsiʿ,[47] which was like the face of a bereaved mother." Mālik ibn Anas ﵀ said, "Whenever I felt any hardness in my heart, I would go to Muḥammad ibn al-Munkadir[48] and take one glance at him, and that would keep me admonished for days." The passing of time here might also refer to inclining toward the world and turning away from circles of invocation and counsel, which clearly has a hardening effect upon the heart. It may also refer to a long time spent in heedlessness.

In sum, straying from the revealed Law and its people, and from righteous folk in general, causes the heart to harden, to become emboldened to violate God's boundaries, and to lose the sense of reverence for God's sacred waymarks. That is why God Most High links veneration of His waymarks with the reverence (*taqwā*) of the heart, saying, *So it is; and whosoever venerates God's sacred waymarks, truly that comes from reverence in the heart* [Qur'ān 22:32].

That is just what happened to the People of the Book, who forgot the rulings of the revealed Law when they departed from it and they became heedless and felt safe from punishment. As the saying goes, "He who feels safe from punishment will misbehave." So once they acted like that, their hearts hardened and became emboldened to violate God's boundaries and play games with His Decrees. God Most High describes this by saying, *Then in their wake came successors who inherited the Book. They choose the transient things of this lower world and say, "It will be forgiven us;" yet if such transient things were to come to them again, they would still take them* [Qur'ān 7:169].

The many other lessons of this verse include:

(1) The verse illustrates how "familiarity breeds contempt." Just as distance causes the heart to harden, closeness can lead to mundanity,

---

47: Muḥammad Ibn Wāsiʿ al-Azdī (d. 127/745) was a hadith narrator and ascetic from the generation of the Followers.

48: Muḥammad ibn al-Munkadir (d. 130/747) was a Medinan narrator from the generation of the Followers.

أنس رضي الله عنه: "كنتُ إذا وجدتُ من قلبي قسوة آتي محمد بن المُنْكَدِر فأنظرَ إليه نظرة فأتعظُ بها أياماً." وقد يكون المراد من طول الأمد الميل للدنيا والإعراض عن مجالس الذكر والمواعظ وهو واضح الأثر في قسوة القلوب. وقد يكون المراد به طول المدة في الغفلة.

والخلاصة، أنَّ البعد عن الشرع وأهله والصالحين عموما يورث القلب قسوة واجتراء على محارم الله وفقدان تعظيم شعائر الله. ولذلك ربط الله تعالى تعظيم الشعائر بتقوى القلوب فقال: "**ذَٰلِكَ وَمَنْ يُعَظِّمْ شَعَائِرَ اللَّهِ فَإِنَّهَا مِنْ تَقْوَى الْقُلُوبِ**" (الحج: ٣٢)

وقَد هذا وقَعَ لأهل الكتاب، حيث أنهم نسوا أحكام الشرع ببعدهم عنها وغفلتهم وأمنوا العقاب. وقد قيل: من أمن العقاب أساء الأدب. فلما وقع هذا منهم، قست قلوبهم واجترأت على حدود الله والتلاعب بأحكامه. وقد وصف الله تعالى هذا فقال: "**خَلَفَ مِنْ بَعْدِهِمْ خَلْفٌ وَرِثُوا الْكِتَابَ يَأْخُذُونَ عَرَضَ هَٰذَا الْأَدْنَىٰ وَيَقُولُونَ سَيُغْفَرُ لَنَا وَإِنْ يَأْتِهِمْ عَرَضٌ مِثْلُهُ يَأْخُذُوهُ.**" (الأعراف: ١٦٩)

وفي الآية فوائد جمةٌ غير ما أسلفناه منها:

(١) أنَّ الآية أفادت أيضا أن الألفة ترفع الكلفة، فكما أن البعد يورث القسوة فالقرب المؤدي للاعتياد ينزع الهيبة. فالمجترءون على الأحكام إما باغ جاحد بعيد لا يأبه للشرع ولا يلتزمه أصلا فليس للشرع في قلبه توقير أو ممارس لظاهره مثل بعض العارفين بالرقوم الآخذين بالرسوم المتجاهلين لمرامي الشرع ومعانيه. وقد قيل: "إنما العلمُ

which dulls the sense of awe. Some of those who are bold enough to violate laws are brazen transgressors who are so distant from the Sacred Law that they do not care about it or feel bound by it in the slightest, their hearts being devoid of any respect for it. Others, however, practice the outward aspects of the Law, such as some of those who acknowledge ceremony and hold to rituals, but ignore the true meaning and purposes of the Law. It has been said that "knowledge is reverential fear;" and if knowledge is not accompanied by such fear, anybody who acquires it and observes its outward form while ignoring its intended effect is in even greater and more serious peril than the one who has strayed far from it. The Proof of Islam al-Ghazālī criticized some of the pharisaical, formalist scholars of his time by saying:

> Our scholars are like the wick of a candle,
> Which burns up while giving people light;
> A foul root beneath a pure exterior,
> Like silver plating applied to brass.

(2) The verse contained a prophecy: the good news that the Community of Islam would have a long life and last for almost as long as, or even longer than, that of the People of the Book. The truth of that prophecy is there for all to see.

الخشية" فإن لم يصحب العلمَ الخشيةُ كان خطر المتعرض للعلم المتقن لظاهره الغائب عن أثره أشد وأعظم من ذلك البعيد. وقد نقد الحجةُ الغزالي بعض العلماء المترسمين في زمانه فقال:

علماؤنا كذبالة النبراس
هي في الحريق وضوؤها في الناس
أصلٌ خبيثٌ تحت رائق منظر
كالفضة البيضاء فوق نحاس

(٢) أن الآية حملت بشرى وهو طول عمر أمة الإسلام إلى مدة تطول قريبا أو أكثر من مدة أهل الكتاب وشاهده قائم حاضر.

Parable 39: Remembrance is the Life of the Heart

Sūrat al-Ḥadīd (57), Verse 17

Know that God revives the earth after its death. We have made the signs clear for you, that you may understand.

This verse presents a parable for hearts which have died due to hardness, likening them to inert and lifeless earth, and the return of life and piety to the heart through remembrance and worship, likening it to the revival of the earth by rain and water.

It is as though this verse provides the solution for the ailment of hard-heartedness to which the previous verse refers. It stresses the faithful heart's need for remembrance by comparing it to the state of dead, dry earth, which is in need of water, and comparing the power of remembrance to purify and elevate the soul with how rain revives parched earth.

The verse is not meant literally as information about the earth being revived by water, because that is something obvious which would not need to be prefaced by the command, *Know*.

The verse contains both an explicit parabolic figure of speech and also an implicit one: it omits mention of the state being compared but does mention its consequence, the revival of the earth, because God revives the earth after its death with rain. It is as though He said, 'Remembrance is like rain', and then omitted mention of the rain but mentioned its consequence, which is the revival of the earth.

المثلُ التاسع والثلاثين: الذكرُ حياة القلوب
سورةُ الحديد الآية (١٧)

﴿ اعْلَمُوا أَنَّ اللَّهَ يُحْيِي الْأَرْضَ بَعْدَ مَوْتِهَا ۚ قَدْ بَيَّنَّا لَكُمُ الْآيَاتِ لَعَلَّكُمْ تَعْقِلُونَ ﴾

مثلت هذه الآية القلوب التي ماتت بسبب القساوة بالأرض الخامدة الهامدة وعودة الحياة والخشوع لها بالذكر والعبادة بإحياء الأرض بالغيث والمطر.

وكأن هذه الآية تحمل الحلَّ لعلة القساوة التي أشارت إليها الآية السابقة وتنبه على حال احتياج القلوب المؤمنة للذكر وافتقارها إليه بتمثيله بحال الأرض الميتة الجافة تحتاج إلى المطر، وحال الذكر في تزكية النفوس وترقيتها بحال الغيث يحي الأرض الجدباء. والآية ليست على ظاهرها من الإخبار بحياة الأرض بالغيث لأنه أمر ظاهر لا يحتاج إلى أن يستفتح بقوله: "اعلموا" والآية تحوي استعارة تمثيلية مصرحة وتتضمن أيضا استعارة تمثيلية مكنية حيث طوى ذكر الحالة المشبه بها وذكّرَ بلازمها وهو احياء الأرض، لأ الله يحي الأرض بعد موتها بسبب المطر فكأنه قال: الذكر كالمطر ثم حذف المطر وذكر لازمه وهو حياة الأرض به.

The subtle points in this verse include:

(1) It alludes to the means of contrition, and encourages exposing the soul to counsels and reminders by turning to and contemplating the Qur'ān and the words of the Messenger of God ﷺ, because taking refuge with both of these provides salvation, and fleeing to them ensures protection.

(2) The verse hints at an underlying meaning, which is that the believer must stand at God's door and beseech Him to restore life to his heart and remove the hardness and covering from it, just as people resort to the prayer for rain when they are beset by drought and famine, knowing that no salvation or rain can come from anyone but God the Exalted.

(3) The verse instils hope into the heart of every sinner, and opens the door to all who have strayed, so that they may return and repent, knowing that God's door is open and that no matter how long it has been and how far they have strayed, life can always return to the heart if it returns to the Restorer (Jabbār) of the heavens and the earth. Imam ʿAbd al-Raḥmān ibn ʿAbd Allāh Balfaqīh speaks of this parable in his *Rashafāt*:

> From the Mercy of the All-Merciful One,
> Breezes of generosity and kindness,
> Constant, abundant, uplift those with defects
> And realize the hopes of those who have hopes.
> Many a hardened sinner they have raised up,
> Many an errant rebel they have rescued;
> Once far off, he became one of the chosen,
> Brought near in triumph, unaided by good deeds!

والآية تحوي لطائف منها:

(١) الإشارة إلى وسيلة الإنابة والحث على تعهد النفس بالموعظة والتذكير بالإقبال على القرآن وتدبره وكلام رسول الله ﷺ وذلك أن في اللجأ إليهما نجاة وفي المفزع إليهما عصمة.

(٢) التلويح بمعني خفي وهو أن المؤمن مطالب أن يقف علي باب الله والضراعة له كي يعيد لقلبه الحياة ويزيل القساوة والغشاوة عنه كما يفزع الناس بصلاة الاستسقاء حين يصيبهم الجدب ويحل بهم القحط وتنزل بهم السنون الشهباء ويعلمون أنه لا نجاة ولا سقيا إلا من عند الله تعالى.

(٣) بثُّ الأملِ في قلبِ كلِّ عاصي وفتح الباب أمام كلِّ قاصي كي يرجع وينيب ويعلم أن باب الله مفتوح وأن الحياة - مهما طال الأمد واستبد البعاد - تعود للقلب إن رجع لجبار السماوات والأرض. وفي مثل هذا يقول الإمام عبد الرحمن بن عبد الله بلفقيه في رشفاته:

فلم تزلْ منْ رحمةِ الرحمن
ونفحات الجود والإحسان
سوابغٌ أَعْلَتْ ذوي نُقْصانِ
وَبَلَّغَتْ آمَالَ ذي آمَال
كَمْ قَرَّبَتْ مِنْ مُعْرِضٍ وَقَاصي
وأَنقَذَت مِنْ زَائِغٍ وَعَاصي
فَصَارَ بعدَ البُعْدِ ذا اختِصَاصِ
وَ فَازَ بالقُربِ بِلا أَعْمَال

Parable 40: Form Without Substance

Sūrat al-Munāfiqūn (63), Verse 4

And when you see them, their figures impress you; and if they speak, you listen to their words. They are like leaning timber beams. They think that every cry is against them. They are the enemy, so beware of them. God confound them! How deviated they are!

This verse likens the Hypocrites, who appeared impressive but were useless, to large pieces of timber leaning against a wall. They are broad, long, and sturdy, but there is no good in them and so they cannot be used in a roof or a wall. Likewise, there were Hypocrites who had imposing strong bodies, honeyed words, and eloquent tongues, and an onlooker might suppose them to be men of intelligence, courage, knowledge, and experience; but if he put them to the test he would find that they were the complete opposite. They were like propped-up boards, form without substance, a façade over a foul interior.

It would appear that this verse does not refer to all of the Hypocrites, as though they were all men of eloquence and physical prowess, since that would be unlikely. Rather, it means certain members of their leadership in particular. This sura describes them at length, explaining some of their traits, the rest of which are mentioned in *Sūrat al-Tawba*. Regarding their impressive appearance, Ibn ʿAbbās

المثلُ الأربعون: صورة ولا حقيقة
سورةُ المنافقون الآية (٤)

﴿وَإِذَا رَأَيْتَهُمْ تُعْجِبُكَ أَجْسَامُهُمْ وَإِنْ يَقُولُوا تَسْمَعْ لِقَوْلِهِمْ كَأَنَّهُمْ خُشُبٌ مُسَنَّدَةٌ يَحْسَبُونَ كُلَّ صَيْحَةٍ عَلَيْهِمْ هُمُ الْعَدُوُّ فَاحْذَرْهُمْ ۚ قَاتَلَهُمُ اللَّهُ أَنَّىٰ يُؤْفَكُونَ﴾

شبهت هذه الآية المنافقين في حُسن مرآهم وعدم جدواهم بالخشب الضخمة المُسندةِ إلى حائطٍ، فهي غليظة طويلة قوية غير أنه لا نفع فيها فلا تستخدم في سقف ولا جدار. وذلك لأنهم كانوا أصحاب أجسام ضخمة قوية وكلام معسول ولسان فصيح يظن الرائي أنهم أرباب لبٍّ وشجاعة وعلم ودراية فإذا اختبرهم وجدهم على خلاف ذلك تماما فهم كالخشب المسندة صورة لا حقيقة لها، وظاهر على باطن خبيث.

والظاهر أنَّ الآية لا تشير لكل المنافقين على أنهم أصحاب فصاحة وجسامة فإنَّ ذلك بعيد وإنما المراد بعضُ أكابرهم ورؤوسهم خاصة وأنَّ هذه السورة بسطت من أخبارهم وشرحت من أحوالهم ما ذُكِرَ باقيه في سورة التوبة. وأما حسنُ الصورة فقد ذكر ابن عباس رضي الله عنهما أنَّ

ﷺ related that ʿAbd Allāh ibn Ubayy[49] was large-framed, fit, eloquent, and silver-tongued. Al-Kalbī[50] said that the verse refers to Ibn Ubayy, Jadd ibn Qays, and Muʿattab ibn Qushayr,[51] who were men of fine stature, good appearance, and eloquence.

The subtleties in this verse which we shall summarize here are as follows:

(1) What matters to God Most High is action and the heart, for "what makes a man are his two smallest parts: his heart and his tongue."[52] Beauty of the body and sweetness of the tongue are of no avail, unless a person is truly as they make him appear to be. Ḥassān ibn Thābit[53] ﷺ said of those whose bodies are rugged but whose minds are weak:

> Not bad, those folk so tall and tough—
> Mules' bodies, and the brains of sparrows!

It is related concerning a number of the Companions, may God be pleased with them all, that they were small-statured and slender-boned. One of them was ʿAbd Allāh ibn Masʿūd ﷺ, who was so slender that a gust of wind might almost have carried him away. The Companions laughed when they saw how thin his shin was, but the Prophet ﷺ said, "On the Day of Resurrection it will be heavier than Mount Uḥud." There were other Companions who were very slender, and some who were not very tall, such as Julaybīb and others. In sum, what matters is the heart and its connection with

---

49: ʿAbd Allāh ibn Ubayy ibn Salūl (d. 9/631) was a chief of the Khazraj tribe and the leader of the hypocrites of Medina.
50: Muḥammad ibn al-Sā'ib al-Kalbī (d. 146/763) was an exegete and genealogist of Kufa.
51: Jadd ibn Qays and Muʿattab ibn Qushayr were among those considered as hypocrites of Medina.
52: An Arab proverb.
53: Ḥassān ibn Thābit (d. 54/674) was a Companion and poet who composed poetry in defense of the Prophet ﷺ with the latter's blessing.

عبد الله بن أُبيّ كان جسيما صحيحا فصيحا ذلق اللسان. وقال الكلبي: المراد في الآية ابنَ أُبيّ والجدَّ بن قيس ومعتب بن قشير حيث كانت لهم أجسام ومنظر وفصاحة.

وفي الآية لطائف نجمل منها:

(١) الإشارة إلى أن العبرة عند الله تعالى بالعمل والقلب وإنما المرء بأصغريه قلبه ولسانه. وأما طلاوة الجسم وحلاوة اللسان فلا يفيدان إلا من كانت حقيقته على وفق ذلك. وقد قال حسان بن ثابت رضي الله عنه في من كان جسمه غليظا وعقله خفيفا:

لا بَأس بالقَوْمِ مِنْ طُوْلٍ وَمِنْ غِلَظٍ
جِسْمُ البِغَالِ وأَحْلَامُ العَصَافِيرِ

وقد جاء عن جماعة من الصحابة -رضوان الله عليهم أجمعين- أنهم كانوا صغار الأجسام دقاق العظام، فمنهم عبد الله بن مسعود -رضي الله عنه- كان من دقة جسده تكاد الريح أن تُطَيِّرَهُ حتى إن الصحابة ضحكوا لما شاهدوا من حموشة أي دقة ساقيه فقال النبي ﷺ إنهما يوم القيامة أثقل من جبل أُحُد. وكان غيره من الصحابة نحاف الجسم وبعضهم لم يكن بذي هيئة مثل جليبيب وغيره. والخلاصة أن المعول على القلب واتصاله بالله وأن قيمة الإنسان بعمله. وقد جاء من أخبار كثير من العلماء أنهم كانوا أصحاب خلقة دميمة لكن يعلوهم نور العلم، بل ربما نظر إليهم الناظر شزرا فلما انكشف له ما احتوت

God, and a person's value lies in his deeds. It has been related that many of the ulama had unattractive features, but they were elevated by the light of knowledge. Sometimes a visitor might look askance at them, but once it became evident to him what mighty souls those bodies contained, he could not fail to yield and surrender to them. Some of them had no worldly standing or nobility at all, but since they possessed knowledge and piety, they ascended to high stature and immense importance.

It is related that the eminent Follower and great jurist 'Aṭā' ibn Abī Rabāḥ ﷺ had been a slave belonging to a woman of Mecca, and he was black and disfigured with a nose like a broad bean. Then he pursued knowledge and attained glory and status through it, until the caliph Sulaymān ibn 'Abd al-Malik[54] himself stopped to ask him about the pilgrimage rites. Al-Khaṭīb al-Baghdādī[55] said, 'Muḥammad ibn 'Abd al-Raḥmān al-Awqaṣ had a short neck and protruding shoulders like pikes. Then he pursued knowledge and served as judge of Mecca for twenty years. When any party in a lawsuit sat before him, he would tremble in awe of his erudition.' Much more of the same kind could be said, but this is sufficient for any reflective person.

(2) God compares the Hypocrites to propped-up pieces of timber for two reasons. One is that when wood is left unused, this indicates that it is of no use, since it has not been used in a wall, a roof, or anything else. The second is that it may refer to idols carved from wood, which were well-formed but of no benefit. Also, timber leaning against a wall has one end facing one way and the other facing the other, which was just how they were, for they displayed one thing and concealed another. What is more, the final end of timber is to be burned as firewood—which will also be their final destiny. May God save us from such an evil destiny!

54: Sulaymān ibn 'Abd al-Malik (d. 99/717) was the seventh Umayyad caliph.
55: Abū Bakr ibn 'Alī al-Khaṭīb al-Baghdādī (d. 463/1071) was a narrator and historian.

عليه أجسامهم من نفوس كبيرة ما استطاع إلا أن يذعن ويسلم. بل كان بعضهم ليس بذي منزلة ولا شرف فلما حوى العلم والتقوى علا مكان وعز شانا.

وقد جاء عن عطاء بن أبي رباح - رضي الله عنه- التابعي الجليل والفقيه العظيم أنه كان مملوكا لامرأة من أهل مكة وكان أسود مستوحش الخلقة كأنَّ أنفه باقلاه، فتعلم العلم فنال به العز والرفعة حتى وقف سليمان بن عبد الملك - وهو خليفة يسأله عن المناسك. وذكر الخطيب البغدادي: كان محمد بن عبد الرحمن الأوقص - عُنُقُه داخلاً في بدنه وكان منكباه خارجين كأنهما زُجَّان (أي سهمان أو رمحان) فطلب العلم فَوُلِّي قضاء مكة عشرين سنة ، قال : فكان الخصم إذا جلس بين يديه يُرْعَدُ من هيبته لأجل علمه. والحديث في مثل هذا يطول وفي هذا لمن يعقل كفاية.

(٢) إنما شبههم بالخشب المسندة من جهتين؛ الأولى أن الخشب إذا تُرِكَ دلَّ على خلوه من فائدة حيث لم ينتفع به في جدار ولا سقف أو غيرهما، والثانية أن يكون المراد بها الأصنام المنحوته من خشب في حسن الصورة وعدم الجدوى. ثم إنَّ الخشب المسند للحائط أحد طرفيه إلى جهة والآخر إلى جهة أخرى وكذلك حالهم فهم يظهرون شيئا ويبطنون آخر. فضلا عن ذلك فمآل الخشب أن يكون حطبا يحترق وكذلك مآلهم أعاذنا الله من شر ذلك المآل.

Conclusion

Praise be to God, Who has granted bounty, favor, generosity, and fruition. May God exalt and preserve our master Muḥammad and his Companions.

One of God's favors to His servants is to grant them time and extend their lives long enough for them to complete their tasks, and to finish what He permitted them to begin. God Most High has allowed me, His needy servant, to complete this compilation with perfect kindness and wellbeing from Him. I ask Him to complete His bounty and grant this work acceptance, and to make it a contribution to the understanding of the Book of God Most High, and a means of bringing out one aspect of the beauty of this wise and miraculous Book. I seek forgiveness from God for any errors or shortcomings. I hope that the reader will graciously offer counsel, advice, and direction, for perfection is not easily achieved. I ask God Most High to place the reward for this labor in the register of our master Muḥammad the Messenger of God ﷺ, his Family, my parents, my teachers, my wife, my children, my students, and my dear friends. May He place us all where He approves for us to be. As usual, I will conclude with these lines, with which God graced me upon the completion of the book without any prior thought or planning on my part. I say, therefore:

> The Book of God contains enlightening parables,
> Which edify all those possessed of fine minds.
> Their meaning is clear, their wisdom abundant

الخاتمة

الحمد لله الذي تفضل وأنعم وأكرم وتمم وصلى الله على سيدنا محمد وآله وصحبه وسلم وبعد فمن نعم الله تعالى أن يُفسح لعبده في الوقت ويبسط له في الأجل كي يتمم أعماله ويختم ما أذن الله له بالبدء فيه وقد يسر الله تعالى أن أختم هذا المجموع والفقير في تمام لطف وعافية من الله تعالى.

وإني أسأله تعالى أن يتم فضله فيجعل القبول نصيبه ويقبله لبنة من اللبنات المعينة على فهم كتاب الله عز وجل واظهار جانب من جوانب جمال هذا الكتاب المعجز الحكيم. وأستغفر الله من كل خلل أو قصور، وأرجو من القارئ أن يتفضل بالنصح والتوجيه والإشارة فإدراك الكمال عزيز المنال. وأسأل الله تعالى أن يجعل ثواب هذا العمل في ديوان سيدنا رسول الله ﷺ وآل بيته ووالداي وأشياخي وزوجي وأولادي وطلابي وأحبابي وأن يقيمنا جميعا فيما يرضيه وأختم - كما عودت القارئ - بهذه الأبيات التي أنعم الله بها في ختام الكتاب دون سبق تعمّل أو ترتيب، فقلت:

في كتاب الله أمثال تضي
يستقيها كلُّ ذي عقل رضي

Yet obscure to the misled and the biased.
Their light streams forth, with guidance to high places,
For all, be they near or far and disdainful.
In this book of mine I've made a selection,
That may perhaps inspire a heart that's beating.
I've done no more than to unravel in them
Less obvious points my mind struggled to master.
I ask forgiveness for my sins, and that my Lord
Protect me from any hate-filled enemy.
And may God's blessings enfold the Chosen One,
As long as bountiful clouds pour the rain down.

Completed on Wednesday the 24th of Rabīʿ al-Awwal, 1439, corresponding to the 12th of December 2017, in my study in Birmingham, may God make it always a place of security, safety, and peace. Praise be to God, first and last.

جلَّ معناها وفاضت حكمة
غاب عنها كلُّ غِرٍّ مُغرض
نورها يسري فيهدى للعلا
كلَّ دانٍ أو بعيد معرضِ
صغت منها في كتابي جملةً
علها تدنو لقلبٍ نابضِ
لم أزد فيها على فكِّ لما
كلَّ عقلي أن يرى -من غامضِ
سائلا غفران ذنبي وكذا
حفظ ربي من عدوٍّ مُبغض
وصلاة الله تغشى المصطفى
ما همى بالغيث جودُ العارضِ

وقد فاح مسك ختامها يوم الثلاثاء ٢٤ من ربيع الأول سنة ١٤٣٩ ه الموافق ٢١ من ديسمبر ٢٠١٧ م بمكتبتي العامرة ببرمنكهام - أدامها الله منزل أمن وسكينة وسلام والحمد لله أولا وآخرا.

Bibliography

The Holy Qur'ān.

Abūl-ʿAtāhiyya, Ismāʿīl ibn al-Qāsim. *Dīwān*. Beirut, 2009.

Azharī, Ahmed Saad al-. *Contemplating the Quran: A Thematic Thirty-Part Commentary on the Noble Quran*. [London], 2017.

Ājurrī, Muḥammad ibn al-Ḥusayn al-. *Akhlāq al-ʿulamāʾ*. Riyadh, 2005.

ʿAlī ibn Abī Ṭālib. *Dīwān*. Beirut, 2010.

ʿAskarī, Abū Hilāl Ḥasan ibn Sahl al-. *Jamharat al-amthāl*. Cairo, 1964.

Bilfaqīh, ʿAbd al-Raḥmān ibn ʿAbd Allāh. *Rashafāt ahl al-kamāl wa-nasamāt ahl al-wiṣāl*. Tarīm, 2015.

Bukhārī, Muḥammad ibn Ismāʿīl al-. *al-Jāmiʿal-Ṣaḥīḥ*. Dār al-Minhaj 3rd ed. Jeddah, 2015.

al-Adab al-mufrad. Beirut, 2022.

Dhahabī, Shams al-Dīn Muḥammad ibn Aḥmad al-. *Siyar aʿlām al-nubalāʾ*. Beirut, 1996.

Fīrūzābādī, Majd al-Dīn Muḥammad ibn Yaʿqūb al-. *al-Qāmūs al-muḥīṭ*. Cairo, 2010.

Ḥabashī, ʿAlī ibn Muḥammad al-. *Dīwān al-Sirr al-maṣūn wal-Jawhar al-maknūn*. Beirut, 1433/2012.

Ḥaddād, ʿAbd Allāh ibn ʿAlawī al-. *Dīwān, al-musammā al-Durr al-manẓūm li-dhawī al-ʿuqūl wal-fuhūm*, 2001.

Ḥākim al-Nīsābūrī, Muḥammad ibn ʿAbd Allāh al-. *al-Mustadrak ʿalā al-Ṣaḥīḥayn*. Beirut, 2006.

Ḥakīm al-Tirmidhī, Muḥammad ibn ʿAlī al-. *al-Amthāl min al-Kitāb*

المراجع

القرآن الكريم
كتب السنة (البخاري - مسلم - الترمذي - الطبراني وغيرها)
تفسير التحرير والتنوير للطاهر بن عاشور
تفسير الكشاف لجار الله الزمخشري
التفسير الكبير للفخر الرازي
تفسير لطائف الإشارات لأبي القاسم القشيري
تفسير البحر المديد لأحمد بن عجيبة الحسني
تفسير جامع البيان للطبري
أخلاق العلماء للآجري
سير أعلام النبلاء للإمام الذهبي
القاموس المحيط لمجد الدين الفيروزآبادي
تاج العروس للمرتضى الزبيدي
رشفات أهل الكمال ونسمات أهل الوصال لعبد الرحمن بن عبد الله بلفقيه
ديوان الإمام الحداد
ديوان سيدنا علي بن أبي طالب
ديوان أبي العتاهية
ديوان السر المصون والجوهر المكنون للإمام علي بن محمد بن حسين الحبشي
جمهرة الأمثال لأبي هلال العسكري
الكليات لأبي البقاء الكفوي

wal-Sunna. Cairo, 1975.

Ibn ʿAjība, Aḥmad ibn Muḥammad. *Tafsīr al-Baḥr al-madīd*. Beirut, 2005.

Ibn ʿĀshūr, Muḥammad al-Ṭāhir ibn Muḥammad. *Tafsīr al-Taḥrīr wal-Tanwīr*. Tunis, 1984.

Kafawī, Abūl-Baqāʾ al-. *Kulliyyāt*. Damascus, 2012.

Muḥammad ibn ʿAbd al-Raḥīm al-Mullā. *Miftaḥ al-qurb fī sharḥ manẓūmat Ādāb al-akl wal-shurb*. Al-Aḥṣā, 2012.

Muslim ibn al-Ḥajjāj. *al-Jāmiʿal-Ṣaḥīḥ*. Jeddah, 2013.

Qushayrī, Abūl-Qāsim ʿAbd al-Karīm ibn Hawāzin al-. *Tafsīr al-Qushayrī al-musammā Laṭāʾif al-ishārāt*. 2nd ed. Beirut, 2007.

Rāzī, Fakhr al-Dīn, Muḥammad ibn ʿUmar al-. *al-Tafsīr al-kabīr*. Beirut, 2005.

Suyūṭī, Jalāl al-Dīn al-. *al-Durr al-manthūr fīl-tafsīr bil-manthūr*. Cairo, 2003.

Ṭabarānī, Sulaymān ibn Aḥmad al-. *al-Muʿjam al-awsaṭ*. Cairo, 1995.

Ṭabarī, Muḥammad ibn Jarīr al-. *Jāmiʿ al-bayān ʿan taʾwīl āy al-Qurʾān*. Amman, 2002.

Tirmidhī, Muḥammad ibn ʿĪsā al-. *Jāmiʿ*. Al-Maknaz ed. [Vaduz], 2000.

Zabīdī, Murtaḍā Muḥammad ibn Muḥammad al-. *Tāj al-ʿarūs*. Kuwait, 1975.

Zamakhsharī, ʿUmar ibn Maḥmūd al-. *Tafsīr al-Kashshāf*. Riyadh, 1998.

مفتاح القرب في شرح منظومة آداب الأكل والشرب لمحمد بن عبد الرحيم الملا

www.ingramcontent.com/pod-product-compliance
Lightning Source LLC
Chambersburg PA
CBHW070134080526
44586CB00015B/1691
9781939256249